Bill HEATH
42 Bedford Rd.,
Sandy
BEDFORDSHIRE
U.K.
SG19 1EW
01767683628

Churches beware!

Churches beware!

Warnings to the churches

J. C. Ryle

EVANGELICAL PRESS

EVANGELICAL PRESS
Grange Close, Faverdale North Industrial Estate, Darlington,
Co. Durham, DL3 0PH, England

This selection of Ryle's writings was first published under the title
of *Warnings to the Churches* by the Banner of Truth Trust in 1967.

This new edition first published 1998

British Library Cataloguing in Publication Data available

ISBN 0 85234 419 8

Unless otherwise indicated, Scripture quotations in this publication
are from the Holy Bible, New King James Version. Copyright ©
1984 by Thomas Nelson Inc. All rights reserved.
    Scripture quotations marked 'AV' are from the Authorized/King
James Version.

Printed and bound in Great Britain by Creative Print and Design,
Ebbw Vale.

Contents

J. C. Ryle

John Charles Ryle first saw the light of day on 10 May 1816 in the county of Cheshire, England. His father, a banker and politician, was an extremely wealthy man, having inherited a fortune derived from the silk-trade. As a young boy and teenager Ryle had a great passion for cricket, and he went on to play for the Oxford University team for three seasons. He also excelled in his studies at Oxford, winning the coveted Craven Scholarship in 1836 and graduating in 1838 with such a high standing that it was said that he, along with two other men, might well have been placed in a class by themselves.

Nevertheless, despite his family wealth, athletic prowess and outstanding academic achievements, the one thing needful for a human being was completely absent from his life. He had no knowledge of God or the way of salvation. His home held the things of God in genuine respect, but vital Christianity was something with which none of his family were acquainted. After his conversion, Ryle would later state of these years: 'I certainly never said my prayers or read a word of my Bible from the time I was seven to the time I was twenty-one.'

It was in mid-summer 1837 that God began to draw Ryle to himself, when a severe illness drove him to the study of the Scriptures and to prayer. Early the following year Ryle found himself seated in an Oxford church listening to the reading of

Ephesians 2. Verse 8 of that chapter, 'For by grace are ye
saved through faith; and that not of yourselves: it is the gift of
God,' was driven home to his heart by God and there in that
church he came to see that the way of salvation is by faith
alone in the atoning work of Christ on the cross. It was a text
that gave him a lifelong love for what are known as the doctrines of grace.

After graduation Ryle returned home to Cheshire, hoping
to go into politics and follow in his father's footsteps. But in
June 1841, all of Ryle's earthly plans were dashed to the ground
when his father went bankrupt and the entire family fortune of
more than half a million pounds, Ryle's inheritance, was lost
overnight. More than thirty years later, Ryle could still recall
with vividness the events of that day: 'We got up one sum-
mer's morning with all the world before us as usual, and went
to bed that same evening completely and entirely ruined.' This
financial catastrophe played a major role in convincing Ryle
that God was calling him to pastoral ministry.

He was ordained that December and over the next thirty-
nine years served a number of parish churches with great distinction. It was in one of these churches, that of Helmingham,
Suffolk, where he ministered from 1844 to 1861, that Ryle
soaked his mind and heart in the writings of the Reformers
and the Puritans. The solid, doctrinal core of their teaching,
united to their profound devotion to the Lord Jesus Christ,
gave Ryle a priceless quarry in which to work for the rest of
his life. Little wonder that in his later years he could castigate
many of his fellow Anglicans for their 'jellyfish' Christianity:
'No dogma, no distinct tenets, no positive doctrine.'

It was also in this parish that he began to write tracts. In all
he would write well over two hundred of them, some of them
on historical topics like *Baxter and His Times* — which dealt
with the Puritan author Richard Baxter — but most of them
distinctly evangelistic, with titles like *Are you Forgiven?*, *Are*

you Regenerate?, *Consider your Ways*, *Have you the Spirit?*, *Only One Way*, *Repent or Perish!*, *Shall you be Saved?* It has been reckoned that more than twelve million copies of these tracts, in various languages, were distributed during Ryle's lifetime.

An idea of their influence can be gleaned from an account about one of them, entitled *True Liberty*, that was translated into Spanish and found its way into the hands of a Dominican friar in Mexico. It led to his conversion and ultimately to the growth of a church body reportedly 50,000 strong. It was not without reason, therefore, that Ryle was sometimes called 'the Prince of Tract-Writers'.

In addition to these tracts, Ryle also penned a number of books that set forth the evangelical position over against two extremes: Anglo-Catholicism, the misguided interest in ritual and ceremony in worship that gripped a significant number of Anglicans in the mid-nineteenth century; and liberalism, which began on the European continent and subsequently infected most of the theological schools in the United Kingdom. His best-known book is probably *Knots Untied*, in which chapters 4-8 of this collection were first published, and which details where Anglican evangelicalism stands on various disputed issues. His *Expository Thoughts on the Gospels*, issued in seven volumes between 1856 and 1859, are still of great value, especially with regard to their devotional emphasis.

The crowning years of Ryle's ministry came in the last two decades of the century when he was made the first Bishop of Liverpool in 1880. During his time as bishop, thirty-six new parishes were created in his sphere of spiritual jurisdiction and ninety new church buildings erected. He served the diocese of Liverpool with unabated vigour until his final illness in the autumn of 1899. Enormous reserves of physical strength enabled him to labour for Christ almost up to the very end of his earthly life, which came on 10 June 1900.

A passage from one of his tracts, *Do You Confess?*, well captures the Christ-focused and cross-centred nature of his sturdy evangelicalism: 'Reader, beware of ever losing sight of Christ's priestly office. Glory in his atoning death. Honour him as your substitute and surety on the cross. Follow him as your Shepherd. Hear his voice as your prophet. Obey him as your King. But in all your thoughts about Christ, let it be often before your mind, that he alone is your High Priest.'

Michael Haykin

Preface

For more than a century, J. C. Ryle was the leader of the evangelical party in the Church of England. His policy was to encourage the conservative men to remain in the church rather than to abandon ship and leave the liberals to pursue their programme unhindered.

J. C. Ryle is best known for his plain and lively writings on practical and spiritual themes. His great aim, in all his ministry, was to encourage strong and serious Christian living. But Ryle was not naïve in his understanding of how this should be done. He recognized that, as a pastor of the flock of God, he had a responsibility to guard Christ's sheep and to warn them whenever he saw approaching dangers. His penetrating comments are as wise and relevant today as they were when he first wrote them. While his love for the Church of England shines through all his preaching and writing, his fearless proclamation of biblical truths, his insight into the dangers threatening the church and his practical wisdom are of great value for all Christians, whatever their church background. His sermons and other writings have been consistently recognized, and their usefulness and impact have continued to the present day, even though some of the author's original language has become outdated.

Why, then, should expositions already so successful and of such stature and proven usefulness require adaptation, revision, or even editing? The answer is obvious: to increase their usefulness to today's reader, the language in which they were originally written needs updating. Though his sermons have served other generations well, just as they came from the pen of the author in the nineteenth century, they still could be lost to present and future generations, simply because, to them, the language is neither readily nor fully understandable.

In presenting this new version of Ryle's work to the modern reader, editing of the original text has been kept to a minimum. A few archaic sentence structures and expressions have been omitted or replaced with more modern equivalents. Specific references to the timing of events in relation to the time when Ryle was speaking or writing have been updated. A few obscure references to people or events unlikely to be familiar to the reader have been dropped, or in other cases some additional words of explanation have been added either in the text or in a footnote. Ryle's language abounds with biblical quotations and allusions, with which the reader may not always be familiar, and a small number of additional Bible references have therefore also been inserted at appropriate points in the text to assist the reader in recognizing and understanding such passages. In addition to these changes a few headings have been inserted, based closely on Ryle's own division of his subject matter.

The earlier chapters in this volume were originally given as sermons. Specific references in the text to the congregation present when the sermon was preached have been omitted and the relevant passages amended to reflect the fact that the message is now being presented in a written form. Others were originally published as separate tracts, or 'papers'. In these cases a slight amendment of the wording has been made to take account of the fact that they are no longer separate papers, but chapters in a book.

Throughout the aim has been to make the preaching and writing of Ryle more accessible to the modern reader while retaining its original character. Care has been taken not to distort Ryle's meaning or intent. Bible references are taken from the Holy Bible, New King James Version, except in a few cases where the use of an alternative version conveys more accurately Ryle's understanding and exposition of the Bible text.

Tony Capoccia

1.
The true church

'On this rock I will build my church, and the gates of Hades shall not prevail against it' (Matt. 16:18).

We live in a world in which all things are passing away. Kingdoms, empires, cities, institutions, families — all are liable to change and corruption. One universal law seems to prevail everywhere. In all created things there is a tendency to decay.

There is something sad and depressing in this. What profit does a man have in the labour of his hands? Is there nothing that shall stand? Is there nothing that shall last? Is there nothing that shall endure? Is there nothing of which we can say, 'This shall continue for evermore'? You have the answer to these questions in the words of our text. Our Lord Jesus Christ speaks of something which shall continue, and not pass away. There is one created thing which is an exception to the universal rule to which I have referred. There is one thing which shall never perish and pass away. That thing is the building founded upon the rock — the church of our Lord Jesus Christ. He declares, in the words of our text, 'On this rock I will build my church, and the gates of Hades shall not prevail against it.'

There are five things in these words which demand your attention:

1. A building: 'My church'.
2. A Builder: Christ says, 'I will build my church.'
3. A foundation: 'On this rock I will build my church.'

4. Perils implied: 'The gates of Hades' (AV, 'the gates of hell').

5. Security asserted: 'The gates of Hades (AV, 'hell') shall not prevail against it.'

May God bless our consideration of this passage. May we all search our own hearts and know whether or not we belong to this one church. May we all be stimulated to reflect and to pray!

1. The building

First, you have a 'building' mentioned in the text. The Lord Jesus Christ speaks of 'my church'.

Now what is this church? Few enquiries can be made of more importance than this. For want of due attention to this subject, the errors that have crept into the church, and into the world, are neither few nor small.

The church of our text is no material building. It is no temple made with hands, of wood, or brick, or stone, or marble. It is a company of men and women. It is no particular visible church[1] on earth. It is not the Eastern church or the Western church. It is not the Church of England, or the Church of Scotland — much less is it the church of Rome. The church of our text is one that makes far less show in the eyes of man, but is of far more importance in the eyes of God.

The church of our text is made up of all true believers in the Lord Jesus Christ. It comprehends all who have repented of sin, and fled to Christ by faith, and been made new creatures in him. It comprises all God's elect, all who have received

---

1. Ryle uses the term 'visible church' to refer to the professing Christian church as a whole, whether in a particular location, or denominational group, or worldwide, as distinct from those who make up the true church of Christ, as defined in this chapter.

God's grace, all who have been washed in Christ's blood, all who have been clothed in Christ's righteousness, all who have been born again and sanctified by Christ's Spirit. All such, of every nation, and people, and tongue, compose the church of our text. This is the body of Christ. This is the flock of Christ. This is the bride. This is the Lamb's wife. This is the 'holy catholic church' of which the Apostles' Creed speaks. This is the 'blessed company of all faithful people' spoken of in the Prayer Book. This is the church on the rock.

The members of this church do not all worship God in the same way, or use the same form of government. The 34th Article of the Church of England declares, 'It is not necessary that ceremonies should be in all places one and alike.' But they all worship with one heart. They are all led by one Spirit. They are all really and truly holy. They can all say 'Alleluia', and they can all reply 'Amen'.

This is that church to which all visible churches on earth are servants and helpers. Whether they are Episcopalian, Congregational, or Presbyterian, they all serve the interests of the one true church. They are the scaffolding behind which the great building is carried on. They are the husk under which the living kernel grows. They have their various degrees of usefulness. The best and worthiest of them is that which trains up most members for Christ's true church. But no visible church has any right to say, 'We are the only true church. We are the men, and wisdom shall die with us.' No visible church should ever dare to say, 'We shall stand for ever. The gates of Hades shall not prevail against us.'

This is the church to which belong the Lord's precious promises of preservation, continuance, protection and final glory. To quote Hooker, whatever we read in Scripture, 'concerning the endless love and saving mercy which God [shows] towards his churches, the only proper subject' of these passages 'is this church, which we properly term the mystical body of

Christ'. Small and despised as the true church may be in this
world, it is precious and honourable in the sight of God. The
temple of Solomon in all its glory was lowly and worthless in
comparison with that church which is built upon a rock.

I urge you, dear readers, to see that you hold sound doctrine on the subject of the church. A mistake here may lead on
to dangerous and soul-ruining errors. The church which is made
up of true believers is the church for which those of us who
are ministers are specially ordained to preach. The church which
comprises all who repent and believe the gospel is the church
to which we desire you to belong. Our work is not done, and
our hearts are not satisfied, until you are made new creatures
and are members of the one true church. Outside of this church
there can be no salvation.

2. The Builder

I pass on to the second point, to which I proposed to call your
attention. Our text contains not merely a building, but a Builder.
The Lord Jesus Christ declares, '*I* will build my church.'

The true church of Christ is tenderly cared for by all the
three persons of the blessed Trinity. In the economy of redemption, beyond all doubt, God the Father chooses and God
the Holy Spirit sanctifies every member of Christ's mystical
body. God the Father, God the Son and God the Holy Spirit,
three Persons and one God, co-operate for the salvation of
every saved soul. This is truth which ought never to be forgotten. Nevertheless, there is a special sense in which the help of
the church is the responsibility of the Lord Jesus Christ. He is
particularly and pre-eminently the Redeemer and the Saviour.
Therefore we find him saying in our text, 'I will build; the
work of building is my special work.'

It is Christ who calls the members of the church in due time. They are 'the called of Jesus Christ' (Rom. 1:6).

It is Christ who gives them life: 'The Son gives life to whom he will' (John 5:21).

It is Christ who washes away their sins. He 'loved us and washed us from our sins in his own blood' (Rev. 1:5).

It is Christ who gives them peace: 'Peace I leave with you, my peace I give to you' (John 14:27).

It is Christ who gives them eternal life: 'I give them eternal life, and they shall never perish' (John 10:28).

It is Christ who grants them repentance: 'Him God has exalted to his right hand to be Prince and Saviour, to give repentance...' (Acts 5:31).

It is Christ who enables them to become God's children. 'As many as received him, to them he gave the right to become children of God' (John 1:12).

It is Christ who carries on the work within them when it is begun: 'Because I live, you will live also' (John 14:19).

In short, 'It pleased the Father that in [Christ] all the fulness should dwell' (Col. 1:19). He is the author and finisher of faith. From him every joint and member of the mystical body of Christians is supplied. Through him they are strengthened for duty. By him they are kept from falling. He shall preserve them to the end, and present them faultless before the Father's throne with exceedingly great joy. He is all things, and all in all to believers.

The mighty agent by whom the Lord Jesus Christ carries out this work in the number of his churches is, without doubt, the Holy Spirit. He is the one who applies Christ and his benefits to the soul. He is the one who is ever renewing, awakening, convincing, leading to the cross, transforming, taking out of the world stone after stone and adding it to the mystical building. But the great Chief Builder, who has undertaken to execute the work of redemption and bring it to completion, is the Son of God, the Word who was made flesh. It is Jesus Christ who 'builds'.

In building the true church, the Lord Jesus condescends to use many subordinate instruments. The ministry of the gospel, the circulation of the Scriptures, the friendly rebuke, the word spoken in season, the influence of afflictions in drawing us to God — all, all are means and methods by which his work is carried on. But Christ is the great superintending architect, ordering, guiding, directing all that is done. What the sun is to the whole solar system, that Christ is to all the members of the true church. Paul may plant and Apollos water, but God gives the increase. Ministers may preach and writers may write, but the Lord Jesus Christ alone can build. And unless he builds, the work stands still.

The Lord Jesus Christ displays great *wisdom* as he builds his church. All is done at the right time, and in the right way. Each stone in its turn is put in the right place. Sometimes he chooses great stones, and sometimes he chooses small stones. Sometimes the work goes on fast, and sometimes it goes on slowly. Man is frequently impatient, and thinks that nothing is happening, but man's time is not God's time. A thousand years in his sight are but as a single day. The great Builder makes no mistakes. He knows what he is doing. He sees the end from the beginning. He works by a perfect, unalterable and certain plan. The mightiest conceptions of architects, like Michelangelo and Sir Christopher Wren, are mere trifling child's play, in comparison with Christ's wise counsels concerning his church.

Christ exhibits great *condescension and mercy* in building his church. He often chooses the most unlikely and roughest stones, and fits them into a most excellent work. He despises none, and rejects none, on account of former sins and past transgressions. He delights to show mercy. He often takes the most thoughtless and ungodly and transforms them into polished corners of his spiritual temple.

Christ displays great *power* in building his church. He carries on his work in spite of opposition from the world, the flesh and the devil. In storm and tempest, through times of trouble, silently, quietly, without noise, without disturbance, without excitement, the building progresses, like Solomon's temple. 'I will work,' he declares, 'and none shall reverse it.'

The people of this world take little or no interest in the building of this church. They care little for the conversion of souls. What are broken spirits and penitent hearts to them? It is all foolishness in their eyes. But while the people of this world care nothing, there is joy in the presence of the angels of God. For the preserving of that church, the laws of nature have often been suspended. For the good of that church, all the providential dealings of God in this world are ordered and arranged. For the elect's sake, wars are brought to an end and peace is given to a nation. Statesmen, rulers, emperors, kings, presidents, heads of governments have their schemes and plans, and think them of vast importance. But there is another work going on of infinitely greater significance, for which they are all no more than the axes and saws in God's hands. That work is the gathering in of living stones into the one true church. How little we are told in God's Word about unconverted men compared with what we are told about believers! The history of Nimrod, the mighty hunter, is dismissed in a few words. The history of Abraham, the father of the faithful, occupies several chapters. Nothing in Scripture is so important as the concerns of the true church. The world takes up little space in God's Word. The church and its story take up much.

Let us for ever thank God, my dear readers, that the building of the one true church is laid on the shoulders of one who is mighty. Let us praise God that it does not rest upon man.

Let us thank God that it does not depend on missionaries, ministers, or committees. Christ is the almighty Builder. He will carry on his work, though nations and visible churches do not know their duty. Christ will never fail. What he has undertaken he will certainly accomplish.

3. The foundation

I pass on to the third point which I proposed to consider — the foundation on which this church is built. The Lord Jesus Christ tells us, '*On this rock* I will build my church.'

What did the Lord Jesus Christ mean, when he spoke of this foundation? Did he mean the apostle Peter, to whom he was speaking? I think most certainly not. I can see no reason, if he meant Peter, why he did not say, 'On you I will build my church.' If he had meant Peter, he would have said, 'I will build my church on you,' as plainly as he said, 'I will give you the keys.' No! It was not the person of the apostle Peter, but the good confession which the apostle had just made. It was not Peter, the erring, unstable man, but the mighty truth which the Father had revealed to Peter. It was the truth concerning Jesus Christ himself which was the rock. It was the truth of Christ as the mediator and as the Messiah. It was the blessed truth that Jesus was the promised Saviour, the true surety, the real intercessor between God and man. This was the rock and this was the foundation on which the church of Christ was to be built.

This foundation was laid at a tremendous cost. It was necessary that the Son of God should take our nature upon himself, and in that nature should live, suffer and die, not for his own sins, but for ours. It was necessary that in that nature Christ should go to the grave and rise again. It was necessary that in that nature Christ should go up to heaven, to sit at the right hand of God, having obtained eternal redemption for all his people. No other foundation but this could have borne the weight of that church of which our text speaks. No other foundation could have met the needs of a world of sinners.

That foundation, once obtained, is very strong. It can bear the weight of the sin of all the world. It has borne the weight of all the sins of all the believers who have built on it. Sins of thought, sins of the imagination, sins of the heart, sins of the head, sins which everyone has seen and sins which no one knows about, sins against God and sins against man, sins of all kinds and descriptions — that mighty rock can bear the weight of all these sins and not give way. The mediatorial office of Christ is a remedy which is sufficient for all the sins of all the world.

To this one foundation every member of Christ's true church is joined. In many things believers are disunited and in disagreement. In the matter of their souls' foundation they are all of one mind. They are all built on the rock. Ask where they get their peace and hope and joyful expectation of good things to come. You would find that all flow from that one mighty truth that Christ is the mediator between God and man, and from the office that Christ holds as the High Priest and surety on behalf of sinners.

Here is the point which demands our personal attention. Are we on the rock? Are we really joined to the one foundation? What does that good old theologian Leighton say? 'God has laid this precious stone for this very purpose, that weary sinners may rest upon it. The multitude of imaginary believers lie all around it, but they are none the better for that, any more than stones that lie loose in heaps, near a foundation, but not joined unto it. There is no benefit to us by Christ, without union with him.'

Look to your foundation, my dear readers, if you would know whether or not you are members of the one true church.

It is a point that may be known to yourselves. Your public worship others can see, but they cannot see whether you are personally built on the rock. Your attendance at the Lord's Table others can see, but they cannot see whether you are joined to Christ, and one with Christ, and Christ in you. But all will come to light one day. The secrets of all hearts will be exposed. Perhaps you go to church regularly, you love to take part in the worship and are regular in your attendance and in profiting by all the means of grace your church supplies [that is, church attendance, Bible reading, prayer and so on]. All this is right and good, so far as it goes. But, at the same time, see that you make no mistake about your own personal salvation. See that your own soul is on the rock. Without this, all else is nothing. Without this, you will never stand in the Day of Judgement. Better a thousand times in that day to be found in a humble cottage on the rock, than in a palace on the sand!

4. The implied trials of the church

I proceed, in the fourth place, to speak of the implied trials of the church, to which our text refers. Mention is made there of 'the gates of hell'. By that expression we are to understand the power of the devil!

The history of Christ's true church has always been one of conflict and war. It has been constantly attacked by a deadly enemy, Satan, the prince of this world. The devil hates the true church of Christ with an undying hatred. He is ever stirring up opposition against all its members. He is ever urging the men and women of this world to do his will, and injure and harass the people of God. If he cannot bruise the head, he will bruise the heel. If he cannot rob believers of heaven, he will torment and trouble them on their way to heaven.

For six thousand years this warfare has gone on. Millions of the ungodly have been the devil's agents and done the devil's work, though they were unaware of the fact. The pharaohs, the Herods, Nero, Julian, Diocletian, Mary Tudor and the rest — what were they all, when they persecuted the disciples of Jesus Christ, but the tools of Satan?

Warfare with the powers of hell has been the experience of *the whole body of Christ*. It has always been a bush burning, though not consumed, a woman fleeing into the wilderness, but not swallowed up. The visible churches have their times of prosperity and seasons of peace, but never has there been a time of peace for the true church. Its conflict is perpetual. Its battle never ends.

Warfare with the powers of hell is the experience of *every individual member of the true church*. Each has to fight. What are the lives of all the saints, but records of battles? What were such men as Paul and James and Peter and John and Polycarp and Ignatius and Augustine and Luther and Calvin and Latimer and Baxter, but soldiers engaged in a constant warfare? Sometimes their persons have been attacked, and sometimes their property. Sometimes they have been harassed by being made the objects of misrepresentation and slander, and sometimes by open persecution. But in one way or another the devil has been continually warring against the church. The 'gates of hell' have been continually assaulting the people of Christ.

Dear readers, we who preach the gospel can hold out to all who come to Christ exceedingly great and precious promises. We can offer boldly to you, in our Master's name, the peace of God which passes all understanding. Mercy, free grace and full salvation are offered to everyone who will come to Christ and believe on him. But we promise you no peace with the world, or with the devil. We warn you, on the contrary, that there must be warfare, so long as you are in the body. We would not keep you back, or deter you from Christ's service. But we would have you 'count the cost', and fully understand what Christ's service entails. Hell is behind you. Heaven is before you. Home lies on the other side of a troubled sea. Thousands, tens of thousands have crossed these stormy waters, and in spite of all opposition, have reached the haven where they would be. Hell has attacked them, but has not prevailed. Go forward, dear fellow-believers, and do not be afraid of the adversary. Only abide in Christ, and the victory is sure.

Do not be surprised that the powers of hell are your enemies. 'If you were of the world, the world would love its own' (John 15:19). So long as the world is the world, and the devil the devil, there must be warfare and believers in Christ must be soldiers. The world hated Christ, and the world will hate true Christians, as long as the earth stands. As the great Reformer Luther said, 'Cain will go on murdering Abel so long as the church is on earth.'

Be prepared for the hostility of the powers of hell. Put on the whole armour of God. The tower of David contains a thousand shields, all ready for the use of God's people. The weapons of our warfare have been tried by millions of poor sinners like ourselves, and have never been found to fail.

Be patient in the face of the hostility of the powers of hell. It is all working together for your good. It tends to sanctify. It keeps you awake. It makes you humble. It drives you nearer to the Lord Jesus Christ. It weans you from the world. It helps to make you pray more. Above all, it makes you long for heaven and say, with your heart as well as your lips, 'Come, Lord Jesus.'

Do not be cast down by the hostility of the devil and his followers. The warfare of the true child of God is as much a mark of grace as the inward peace which he enjoys. No cross, no crown! No conflict, no saving Christianity! 'Blessed are

you,' said our Lord Jesus Christ, 'when they revile and perse-
cute you, and say all kinds of evil against you falsely for my
sake.'

5. The security of the true church

There remains one thing more to be considered — the security of the true church of Christ. There is a glorious promise
given by the mighty Builder: 'The gates of hell shall not prevail against it.' He who cannot lie has pledged his royal word
that all the powers of hell shall never overthrow his church. It
shall continue and stand, in spite of every assault. It shall never
be overcome. All other created things perish and pass away,
but not the church of Christ. The hand of outward violence or
the moth of inward decay prevail over everything else, but not
over the church that Christ builds.

Empires have risen and fallen in rapid succession. Egypt,
Assyria, Babylon, Persia, Tyre, Carthage, Rome, Greece, Ven-
ice — where are all these now? They were all the creations of
man's hand, and have passed away, but the church of Christ
lives on. The mightiest cities have become heaps of ruins. The
broad walls of Babylon have sunk to the ground. The palaces
of Nineveh are mounds of dust. The hundred gates of Thebes
are only matters of history. Tyre is a place where fishermen
hang their nets. Carthage is a desolation. Yet all this time the
true church stands. The gates of hell do not prevail against it.

The earliest visible churches have in many cases decayed
and perished. Where are the church of Ephesus and the church
of Antioch? Where are the church of Alexandria and the church
of Constantinople? Where are the Corinthian and Philippian
and Thessalonian churches? Where, indeed, are they all? They
departed from the Word of God. They were proud of their
bishops and synods and ceremonies and learning and antiquity.

They did not glory in the true cross of Christ. They did not hold fast the gospel. They did not give Jesus his rightful office, or faith its rightful place. They are now among the things that have been. Their lampstand has been taken away (Rev. 2:5). But all this time the true church has lived on.

Has the true church been oppressed in one country? It has fled to another. Has it been trampled on and oppressed on one soil? It has taken root and flourished in some other climate. Fire, sword, prisons, fines, penalties have never been able to destroy its vitality. Its persecutors have died and gone to their own place, but the Word of God has lived and grown and multiplied. Weak as this true church may appear to the eye of man, it is an anvil which has broken many a hammer in times past, and perhaps will break many more before the end. He that lays hands on it is touching the apple of God's eye (Zech. 2:8).

The promise of our text is true of *the whole body of the true church*. Christ will never be without a witness in the world. He has had a people in the worst of times. He had seven thousand in Israel even in the days of Ahab. There are some now, I believe, in the dark places of the Roman Catholic and Greek churches who, in spite of much weakness, are serving Christ. The devil may rage horribly. The church may in some countries be brought exceedingly low. But the gates of hell shall never entirely prevail.

The promise of our text is true of *every individual member of the church*. Some of God's people have been brought very low, so that they despaired of their safety. Some have fallen sadly, as David and Peter did. Some have departed from the faith for a time, like Cranmer and Jewell. Many have been tried by cruel doubts and fears. But all have got safely home at last, the youngest as well as the oldest, the weakest as well as the strongest. And so it will be to the end. Can you prevent tomorrow's sun from rising? Can you prevent the tide on the seashore from ebbing and flowing? Can you prevent the planets from moving in their respective orbits? Then, and then alone, can you prevent the salvation of any believer, however feeble — of any living stone in that church which is built on the rock, however small or insignificant that stone may appear.

The true church is *Christ's body*. Not one bone in that mystical body shall ever be broken.

The true church is *Christ's bride*. Those whom God has joined in everlasting covenant shall never be put asunder.

The true church is *Christ's flock*. When the lion came and took a lamb out of David's flock, David rose up and delivered the lamb from his mouth. Christ will do the same. He is David's greater son. Not a single sick lamb in Christ's flock shall perish. He will say to his Father in the last day, 'Those whom you gave me I have kept; and none of them is lost.'

The true church is *the wheat of the earth*. It may be sifted, winnowed, buffeted, tossed to and fro. But not one grain shall be lost. The tares and chaff shall be burned. The wheat shall be gathered into the barn.

The true church is *Christ's army*. The Captain of our salvation loses none of his soldiers. His plans are never defeated. His supplies never fail. When the roll of his soldiers is called at the end the number will be the same as it was at the beginning. Of the men that marched gallantly out of England in the Crimean War, how many never came back! Regiments that went forth, strong and cheerful, with bands playing and banners flying, laid their bones in a foreign land and never returned to their native country. But it is not so with Christ's army. Not one of his soldiers shall be missing at last. He himself declares, 'They shall never perish.'

The devil may cast some of the members of the true church into prison. He may kill, burn, torture and hang. But after he has killed the body, there is nothing more that he can do. He cannot hurt the soul. When the French troops took Rome, they found on the walls of a prison cell under the Inquisition the words of a prisoner. Who he was, we do not know, but his words are worthy of remembrance. Though dead, he still speaks. He had written on the walls, very likely after an unjust trial, and a still more unjust excommunication, the following striking words: 'Blessed Jesus, they cannot cast me out of your true church.' That record is true. Not all the power of Satan can cast out of Christ's true church one single believer.

The people of this world may wage fierce warfare against the church, but they cannot stop the work of conversion. What was it the sneering Emperor Julian said, in the early ages of the church? 'What is the carpenter's son doing now?' An aged Christian answered, 'He is making a coffin for Julian himself.' Only a few months passed away before Julian, with all his pomp and power, died in battle. Where was Christ when the fires of Smithfield were lighted, and when Latimer and Ridley were burnt at the stake? What was Christ doing then? He was still carrying on his work of building. That work will ever go on, even in times of trouble.

Do not be afraid, dear readers, to begin serving Christ. He to whom you commit your souls has all power in heaven and earth, and he will keep you. He will never let you be cast away. Relatives may oppose. Neighbours may mock. The world may slander and sneer. Have no fear! Do not be afraid! The powers of hell shall never prevail against your soul. The one who is for you is greater than all those who are against you.

Do not fear for the church of Christ when ministers die and faithful believers are taken away. Christ can ever maintain his own cause. He will raise up better and brighter stars. The stars are all in his right hand. Leave off all anxious thought about the future. Cease to be cast down by the measures of states-men, or the plots of wolves in sheep's clothing. Christ will ever provide for his own church. Christ will take care that the gates of hell shall not prevail against it. All is going on well, though our eyes may not see it. The kingdoms of this world shall yet become the kingdoms of our God and of his Christ.

A few words of application

Allow me now to give a few words of practical application of this message to my readers. I address many of you for the first time. Perhaps I address many of you for the last time. Let me not conclude without an effort to press home the message to the heart of every reader.

1. Are you a member of the one true church?

My first word of application is to be a question. What shall that question be? How shall I approach you? What shall I ask? I ask you, whether you are a member of the one true church of Christ? Are you in the highest, the best sense, a 'churchman' in the sight of God? You know what I mean. I look far beyond the Church of England. I speak of the church built upon the rock. I ask you, with all solemnity, are you a member of that one church of Christ? Are you joined to the great foundation? Have you received the Holy Spirit? Does the Spirit witness with your spirit, that you are one with Christ, and Christ with you? I plead with you, in the name of God, to lay to heart this question, and to ponder it well.

Pay careful attention to your own state, dear readers, if you cannot give a satisfactory answer to my enquiry. Take care, oh, take care that you do not make shipwreck of your faith. Be on your guard that the gates of hell do not prevail against you at last, that the devil does not claim you as his own and that you are not cast away for ever. Take care that you do not go down to the pit, even from a land where the Bible is known and read and in the full light of Christ's gospel.

2. *An invitation to those who are not yet believers*

My second word of application is to be an invitation. I address
it to all who are not yet true believers. I say to you, 'Come and
join the one true church without delay. Come and join yourselves to the Lord Jesus Christ in an everlasting covenant not
to be forgotten. Come to Christ and be saved.' The day of
decision must come some time. Why not this very day? Why
not today, while it is called today? Why not this very night,
before the sun rises tomorrow morning? Come to him whose
I am and whom I serve. Come to my Master, Jesus Christ.
Come, I say, for all things are now ready. Mercy is ready for
you, heaven is ready for you, angels are ready to rejoice over
you, Christ is ready to receive you. Christ will receive you
gladly and welcome you among his children. Come into the
ark — the flood of God's wrath will soon break upon the
earth — come into the ark and be safe.

Come into the lifeboat. The old world will soon break into
pieces! Do you not hear it creaking? The world is like a wreck
stuck on a sandbank. The night is far spent, the waves are
beginning to rise, the winds are rising; the storm will soon
shatter the old wreck. But the lifeboat is launched, and we, the
ministers of the gospel, plead with you to come into the lifeboat and be saved.

Do you ask, 'How can I come? My sins are so many.' Do
you ask how you shall come? I answer in the words of that
beautiful hymn:

> Just as I am: without one plea,
> But that thy blood was shed for me,
> And that thou bid'st me come to thee,
> O Lamb of God, I come.

That is the way to come to Christ. You should come, waiting
for nothing and delaying for nothing. You should come as a

hungry sinner to be filled, as a poor sinner to be enriched, as a bad, undeserving sinner to be clothed with righteousness. If you come like this, Christ will receive you. 'The one who comes' to Christ, he 'will by no means cast out' (John 6:37). Oh, come, come to Jesus Christ!

3. A word of exhortation to believers

Last of all, let me give a word of exhortation to my believing readers.

Live a *holy* life, dear fellow-believers. Walk worthy of the church to which you belong. Live like citizens of heaven. Let your light shine before men, so that the world may profit by your conduct. Let them know whose you are, and whom you serve. Be epistles of Christ, known and read by all men (2 Cor. 3:2-3), written in such clear letters, that none can say of you, 'I do not know whether that person is a member of Christ or not.'

Live a *courageous* life, dear fellow-believers. Confess Christ before men. Whatever station in life you occupy, in that station confess Christ. Why should you be ashamed of him? He was not ashamed of you on the cross. He is ready to confess you now before his Father in heaven. Why should you be ashamed of him? Be bold. Be very bold. The good soldier is not ashamed of his uniform. The true believer ought never to be ashamed of Christ.

Live a joyful life, dear fellow-believers. Live like those who look for that blessed hope, the Second Coming of Jesus Christ. This is the prospect to which we should all look forward. It is not so much the thought of going to heaven, as of heaven coming to us, that should fill our minds. There is a good time coming for all the people of God, a good time for all the church of Christ, a good time for all believers — a bad time for the impenitent and unbelieving, a bad time for those who will serve their own evil desires and turn their backs on the Lord, but a good time for true Christians. For that good time, let us wait and watch and pray.

The scaffolding will soon be taken down, the last stone will soon be brought out, the top-stone will be placed upon the edifice. Only a little more time, and the full beauty of the building shall be clearly seen. The great Master Builder will soon come himself. A building shall be shown to assembled worlds in which there shall be no imperfection. The Saviour and the saved shall rejoice together. The whole universe shall acknowledge that in the building of Christ's church all was well done.

2.
Not corrupting the Word

'For we are not, as so many, peddling [AV, "which corrupt"] the word of God; but as of sincerity, but as from God, we speak in the sight of God in Christ' (2 Cor. 2:17).

It is no light matter to speak to any immortal souls about the things of God. But the most serious of all responsibilities is to address those who are ministers of the gospel.[1] The awful feeling will come across my mind that one single word wrongly expressed, sinking into some heart and bearing fruit at some future time in some pulpit, may lead to harm of which we cannot know the extent. But there are occasions when true humility is to be seen, not so much in loud professions of our weakness, as in forgetting ourselves altogether. I desire to forget myself in turning my attention to this portion of Scripture, which speaks of the responsibilities of ministers. If I say little about my own sense of insufficiency, do me the justice to believe that it is not because I do not feel it much.

The Greek expression which we have translated as 'corrupt' [AV, or 'peddle', NKJV], is derived from a word, the etymology of which is not quite agreed on by authorities on ancient languages. It either means a tradesman who does his business dishonestly, or a wine-merchant who adulterates the wine which he puts up for sale. Tyndale translates it, 'We are not of those who chop and change the Word of God.' The Rhemish version says, 'We are not as many, who adulterate

---

1. The original sermon on which this chapter is based was delivered at a meeting of clergymen in August 1858.

the Word of God.' In the margin of the Authorized Version we read, 'We are not as many, who deal deceitfully with the Word of God.'

In the construction of the sentence, the Holy Spirit has inspired Paul to use both the negative and the positive way of stating the truth. This mode of construction makes the meaning of the words clear and unmistakable, and gives added intensity and strength to the assertion contained in them. Instances of a similar construction occur in three other remarkable passages of Scripture — two on the subject of baptism, one on the subject of the new birth (John 1:13; 1 Peter 1:23; 3:21). It will be found, therefore, that there are contained in the text both negative and positive lessons for the instruction of the ministers of Christ. Some things we ought to avoid; others we ought to follow.

1. The warnings contained in this passage

The first of the negative lessons is a plain warning against corrupting, or dealing deceitfully with, the Word of God. The apostle says 'many' do it, pointing out to us that even in his time there were those who did not deal faithfully and honestly with God's truth. Here is a full answer to those who assert that the early church was one of unmixed purity. The mystery of lawlessness had already begun to work (2 Thess. 2:7). The lesson which we are taught is to beware of all dishonest ways of presenting the Word of God which we are commissioned to preach. We are to add nothing to it. We are to take nothing away from it.

Now when can it be said of us that we corrupt the Word of God in the present day? What are the rocks and hidden sandbanks which we ought to avoid, if we would not be among the 'many' who deal deceitfully with God's truth? A few suggestions on this topic would be useful.

We corrupt the Word of God most dangerously *when we throw any doubt on the entire and unqualified inspiration of any part of Holy Scripture.*[2] This is not merely corrupting the cup, but the whole fountain. This is not merely corrupting the bucket of living water which we profess to present to our people, but poisoning the whole well. Once wrong on this point, the whole substance of our religion is in danger. It is a flaw in the foundation. It is a worm at the root of our theology. If we once allow this worm to gnaw the root, we must not be surprised if, little by little, the branches, the leaves and the fruit decay. The whole subject of inspiration, I am well aware, is surrounded with difficulty. All I would say is that, in my humble judgement, while recognizing that there are some difficulties which we may not be able now to solve, the only safe and tenable ground to maintain is this: that every chapter and every verse and every word in the Bible has been 'given by inspiration of God' (2 Tim. 3:16). We should never desert a great principle in theology, any more than in science, because of apparent difficulties which we are not able at present to resolve.

Allow me to cite an illustration of this important axiom. Those familiar with astronomy know that before the discovery of the planet Neptune there were difficulties which greatly troubled the most scientific astronomers, respecting certain aberrations of the planet Uranus. These aberrations puzzled the minds of astronomers, and some of them suggested that they might possibly prove the whole Newtonian system to be untrue. But at that time a well-known French astronomer, named Leverrier, read before the Academy of Science a paper in which he laid down this great axiom — that it was not fitting for a scientist to give up a principle because of difficulties which could not be explained. He said in effect, 'We cannot

2. The technical term used by Ryle was 'plenary inspiration', which is still the correct theological term, but may need to be defined for readers less familiar with theological terminology.

explain the aberrations of Uranus now, but we may be sure that the Newtonian system will be proved to be right, sooner or later. Something may be discovered one day which will prove that these aberrations may be accounted for and at the same time the Newtonian system remain true and unshaken.' A few years later, the anxious eyes of astronomers discovered the last great planet, Neptune. This planet was shown to be the true cause of all the aberrations of Uranus, and what the French astronomer had laid down as a principle in science was proved to be wise and true.

The application of the story is obvious. Let us beware of giving up any first principle in theology. Let us not give up the great principle of entire and unqualified inspiration because of difficulties. The day may come when they will all be solved. In the meantime we may rest assured that the difficulties which beset any other theory of inspiration are ten times greater than any which may beset our own.

Secondly, we corrupt the Word of God *when we make defective statements of doctrine.* We do so when we *add to* the Bible the opinions of the church, or of the Fathers, as if they were of equal authority. We do so when we *take away* from the Bible, for the sake of pleasing men or, from a false sense of broad-mindedness, keep back any statement which seems narrow and harsh, or hard. We do so when we try to *soften down* anything that is taught about eternal punishment, or the reality of hell. We do so when we *give a disproportionate emphasis* to certain doctrines. We all have our favourite doctrines, and our minds are so constituted that it is hard to see one truth very clearly without forgetting that there are other truths which are equally important. We must not forget the exhortation of Paul to minister 'in proportion to our faith' (Rom. 12:6). We do so when we exhibit *an excessive anxiety to be evasive* and on our guard and to qualify such doctrines as justification by faith without the deeds of the law, for fear of incurring the charge of antinomianism, or when we flinch from strong statements about holiness, for fear of being thought legalistic. We do so, not least, when we *shrink from the use of Bible language* in giving an account of doctrines. We are apt to keep back such expressions as 'born again', 'election', 'adoption', 'conversion' or 'assurance' and to use a roundabout phraseology, as if we were ashamed of plain Bible words. Space does not permit me to expand on these statements. I simply mention them and leave them for your further consideration.

In the third place, we corrupt the Word of God when we make a defective practical application of it. We do so when we do not discriminate between classes in our congregations — when we address everyone as being possessed of grace, by reason of their baptism or church membership, and do not draw the line between those who have the Spirit and those who have not. Are we not apt to keep back clear, direct appeals to the unconverted? When we have hundreds of persons before our pulpits, a vast proportion of whom we must know are unconverted, are we not apt to say, 'Now if there is any one of you who does not know the things that are necessary for eternal peace…' — when we ought rather to say, 'If there is any one of you who has not received the grace of God'? And are we not in danger of defective handling of the Word in our practical exhortations, by not bringing home the statements of the Bible to the various classes in our congregations? We speak plainly to the poor, but do we also speak plainly to the rich? Do we speak plainly in our dealings with those in positions of power and influence? This is a point on which, I fear, we need to search our consciences.

2. The positive instructions contained in this passage

I now turn to the positive lessons which the text contains: 'As of sincerity … as from God, we speak in the sight of God in Christ.' A few words on each point must suffice.

We should aim to speak *'as of sincerity'* — sincerity of aim, heart and motive; to speak as those who are thoroughly convinced of the truth of what they say; as those who have a deep feeling and tender love for those whom we address.

We should aim to speak *'as from God'*. We ought to strive to feel like men commissioned to speak for God, and on his behalf. In our dread of running into Romanism, we too often forget the language of the apostle: 'I magnify my ministry' (Rom. 11:13). We forget how great is the responsibility of the New Testament minister, and how awful the sin of those who, when a real messenger of Christ addresses them, refuse to receive his message and harden their hearts against it.

We should aim to speak as *'in the sight of God'*. We are to ask ourselves not, 'What did the people think of me?' but, 'What was I in the sight of God?' Latimer was once called upon to preach before Henry VIII and he began his sermon in the following manner (I quote from memory, and do not pretend to verbal accuracy). He began: 'Latimer! Latimer! Do you remember that you are speaking before the high and mighty King Henry VIII, before the one who has power to command you to be sent to prison, before the one who can have your head chopped off, if it pleases him to do so? Won't you be careful to say nothing that will offend royal ears?' Then after a pause, he went on: 'Latimer! Latimer! Don't you remember that you are speaking before the King of kings and Lord of lords — before the one at the bar of whose judgement Henry VIII will stand, before the one to whom one day you will have to give account yourself? Latimer! Latimer! Be faithful to your Master and declare all God's Word.' Oh, that this may be the spirit in which we may always step down from our pulpits — not caring whether men are pleased or displeased, not caring whether men say we were eloquent or a poor speaker, but going away with a conscience which testifies that 'I have spoken as in the sight of God.'

Finally, we should aim to speak *'as in Christ'*. The meaning of this phrase is doubtful. Grotius says, 'We are to speak as in his name, as ambassadors.' But Grotius is a poor authority. Beza says, 'We are to speak about Christ, concerning Christ.' This is good doctrine, but hardly the meaning of the words. Others say, 'We are to speak as being ourselves those who are joined to Christ, as those who have received mercy from Christ, and whose only authority to address others comes from Christ alone.' Others say, 'We should speak as through Christ, in the strength of Christ.' No meaning, perhaps, is better than this. The expression in the Greek exactly corresponds to Philippians 4:13: 'I can do all things through Christ who strengthens me.' Whatever sense we ascribe to these words, one thing is clear: we should speak in Christ, as those who have themselves received mercy; as those who desire to exalt, not themselves, but the Saviour, and as those who do not care at all what men think of them, so long as Christ is magnified in their ministry.

Questions we need to ask ourselves

In conclusion, we should all ask ourselves, 'Do we ever handle the Word of God deceitfully? Do we realize what it is to speak "as from God", as "in the sight of God in Christ"?' Let me put to all preachers a searching question: 'Is there any text in God's Word which we shrink from expounding? Is there any statement in the Bible which we avoid speaking about to our people, not because we do not understand it, but because it contradicts some pet notion of ours as to what is truth?' If this is the case, let us ask our consciences whether we may not be guilty of handling the Word of God deceitfully, or something very like it.

Is there anything in the Bible we keep back for fear of seeming harsh and of giving offence to some of our hearers? Is there any statement, either doctrinal or practical, which we twist the meaning of, which we mutilate or dismember? If so, are we dealing honestly with God's Word?

Let us pray to be kept from corrupting God's Word. Let neither the fear nor the favour of men induce us to keep back, or avoid, or change, or mutilate, or qualify any text in the Bible. Surely we ought to have holy boldness when we speak as ambassadors of God. We have no reason to be ashamed of any statement we make in our pulpits so long as it is scriptural. I have often thought that one great secret of the marvellous honour which God has granted to Mr Spurgeon is the extraordinary boldness and confidence with which he stands up in the pulpit to speak to people about their sins and their souls. It cannot be said he does it from fear of any, or to please any. He seems to treat every class of hearers alike — the rich and the poor, the high and the low, the peer of the realm and the humble farm labourer, the learned and the illiterate. He deals plainly with everyone, according to God's Word. I believe that very boldness has much to do with the success which God is pleased to give to his ministry. Let us not be ashamed to learn a lesson from him in this respect. Let us go and do likewise.

3.
Give yourself entirely to them

'Give yourself entirely to them' (1 Tim. 4:15).

I hardly need to point out that the Greek expression which we have translated, 'Give yourself entirely to them,' is somewhat remarkable. A more literal translation would be: 'Be in these things.' We have nothing exactly corresponding to the expression in our language, and the words which our translators have chosen are perhaps as well calculated as any to convey the idea which was put by the Holy Spirit in Paul's mind.

When the apostle says, 'Give yourself entirely to these things,' he seems to refer to the 'things' of which he had been speaking in the preceding verses, beginning with the words: 'Be an example to the believers in word, in conduct, in love, in spirit, in faith, in purity.'

We have here a target set before the ministers of the New Testament, at which we are all to aim, and which we must all feel that we fall short of. Yet there is an old saying: 'The one who aims high is the one most likely to strike high, and the one who shoots at the moon will shoot further than the man who shoots at the bush.'

The apostle appears to me to suggest that the minister must be a man of one thing; to use his own words, he must be a 'man of God'. We hear of men of business and men of pleasure and men of science. The aim of the minister should be to be 'a man of God', or to employ a phrase sometimes used on the mission-field, to be 'Jesus Christ's man'. An expression is sometimes used with reference to the army, which we may apply to the soldiers of the great Captain of our salvation. Some men are said to have entered the army for the sake of the uniform, and for no other cause. But there are many of whom public opinion says, 'That man is every inch a soldier.' This should be the aim which we should set before ourselves: we should seek to be 'every inch the minister of Jesus Christ'. We should aim to be the same men at all times, in all positions and places, not only on Sunday but also on weekdays, not merely in the pulpit but everywhere — whether in the homes of rich or poor, or by our own fireside. There are those of whom their congregations have said that when they were in the pulpit they never wished them to come out of it, and when they went out they never wished them to go back in. May God give us all grace to take that to heart! May we seek so to live, so to preach, so to work, so to give ourselves entirely to the business of our calling that this bitter remark may never be made about us. Our profession is a very unusual one. Others have their times of relaxation, when they can altogether lay aside their work. This can never be done by the faithful minister of Jesus Christ. Once put on, his office must never be put off. At home, abroad, taking relaxation, going to the seaside, he must always carry his business with him. A great lawyer could say of his official robes, 'Lie there, Lord Chancellor!' That ought never to be the attitude of the minister of Christ.

What the text requires of us

There are some things which the high requirements of this text suggest as needing to be followed after and practised.

The first requirement is for *entire devotion to the great work to which we are ordained*. When one man was commanded by the Saviour to follow him, he replied, 'Lord, let me first go and bury my father,' but then there came that solemn saying: 'Let the dead bury their own dead, but you go and preach the kingdom of God.' Another said, 'Let me first go and bid them farewell who are at my house,' and to him there came the remarkable sentence: 'No one, having put his hand to the plough, and looking back, is fit for the kingdom of God' (Luke 9:59-62). 'Greet no one along the road,' was Christ's charge to the seventy disciples (Luke 10:4). Surely these scriptural expressions teach us that in all that we do in our ministry we must have a high standard. We must strive to be men of one thing — that thing being the work of Jesus Christ.

The second requirement is for *a thorough separation from the things of the world.* I hold it to be of the greatest importance to keep the ministerial office, so far as we can, distinct and separate from everything that is secular. I trust we shall hear every year of fewer and fewer ministers of the gospel who are magistrates, and fewer and fewer ministers who take part in agricultural shows, and win prizes for fat pigs, enormous bulls and large crops of turnips. There is no apostolic succession in such occupations. Nor yet is this all. We should be separated from the pleasures of the world, as well as from its business. There are many innocent and harmless amusements for which the minister of Christ ought to have no time. He ought to say, 'I have no time for these things. I am doing a great work, and I cannot come down.'

The third requirement is for *a jealous watchfulness over our own social conduct.* We ought not to be always making social calls and dining out, as others do. It will not do to say that our Lord went to a marriage feast and sat down to eat in the Pharisee's house, and therefore we may do the same. I only reply, 'Let us go in his spirit, with his faithfulness and boldness, to say a word in season, and to give the conversation a profitable turn, and then we may go with safety.' Unless we do this, we should be careful where we go, with whom we sit down and where we spend our evenings. There was a quaint saying of John Wesley to his ministers, which Cecil quotes, as containing the germ of much truth: 'Don't aim at being thought gentlemen; you have no more to do with being gentlemen than with being dancing-masters.' Our aim should be not to be regarded as agreeable persons at the dinner table, but to be known everywhere as faithful, consistent ministers of Jesus Christ.

The fourth requirement is for *a diligent redemption of time*. We should give attention to reading, every day that we live. We should strive to bring all our reading to bear on our work. We ought to keep our eyes open continually, and be ever picking up material for our sermons — as we travel by the way, as we sit by the fireside, as we are standing on the platform at the railway station. We should be keeping in our mind's eye our Master's business — observing, noting, looking out, gathering up something that will throw fresh light on our work, and enable us to put the truth in a more striking way. The one who looks out for something to learn will always be able to learn something.

What will be the consequences of devoting ourselves to these things?

Having suggested these things, I will next proceed to ask, 'What will be the consequence of our giving ourselves entirely to these things?' Remember, we shall not receive the praise of men. We shall be thought extreme and ascetic and excessively righteous. Those who want to serve God and serve mammon at the same time will think our standard too high, our practice too stringent. They will say that we are going too far and too fast for a world such as that in which we live. May we never care what men say of us, so long as we walk in the

light of God's Word! May we strive and pray to be entirely
independent of, and indifferent to, man's opinion, so long as
we please God! May we remember the woe pronounced by
our Master, when he said, 'Woe to you when all men speak
well of you,' and the words of Paul: 'If I still pleased men, I
would not be a servant of Christ.'

But though in giving ourselves entirely to these things we
shall not win the praise of men, we shall attain the far more
important end of *usefulness to souls*. I acknowledge to the full
the doctrine of the sovereignty of God in the salvation of sinners. I acknowledge that those who preach best and live clos-
est to God have not always been honoured in their lives to the
saving of many souls. But still, the man who is most entirely
and wholly Jesus Christ's man — a man of one thing, who
lives on Sunday and on weekdays, everywhere, at home and
abroad, as a man whose single endeavour is to give himself to
the work of Jesus Christ — this is the man, this is the minister,
who will generally, in the long run, do the most good.

The case of Mr Simeon will apply here. It is a well-known
fact that he was persecuted when he began to testify for Christ
in Cambridge. It is common knowledge that there were many
there who would not speak to him and that the finger of scorn
was pointed at him continually. But we also know that he went
on persevering in the work, and when he died all Cambridge
came out to give him honour, and heads of houses and fellows
of colleges and men who had scoffed at him while he lived
honoured him at his death. They testified that the life he had
lived had had its effect, and that they had seen and known that
God was with him.

I once saw in Dundee someone who had known much of
that godly man, Robert Murray M'Cheyne. She told me that
those who read his letters and sermons had only a very faint
idea of what he was. She said to me, 'If you have read all his
works, you just know nothing at all about him. You must have

seen the man and heard him and known him and have been in
company with him to know what a man of God he was.'

In addition, giving ourselves wholly to these things will
bring *happiness and peace to our consciences.* I am writing as
to friends, and not to worldly people, in which case I should
need to qualify and guard and explain what I mean. I trust that
I shall not be suspected by my readers of holding justification
by works. I speak of such a good conscience as the apostle
refers to when he says, 'We are confident that we have a good
conscience' (Heb. 13:18). To have this good conscience is
clearly bound up with high aims, high motives and a high standard of ministerial life and practice. I am quite sure that the
more we give ourselves entirely to the work of the ministry,
the more inward happiness, the greater sense of the light of
God's countenance we are likely to enjoy.

Following the example of Christ

The subject is a deeply humbling one. Who does not feel, 'Oh,
how worthless, how unprofitable I am! How far short I fall of
this high standard!'? What reason we have, having received
mercy, not to faint! What reason we have, having been spared
by God's long-suffering, to abound in the work of the Lord
and to give ourselves entirely to our business! The grand secret is to be ever looking to Jesus, and living a life of close
communion with him. At Cambridge I saw a picture of Henry
Martyn, bequeathed by Mr Simeon to the public library. A
friend informed me that that picture used to hang in Mr
Simeon's room, and that when he was disposed to trifle in the
work of the ministry, he used to stand before it and say, 'It
seems to say to me, "Charles Simeon, don't trifle, don't trifle.
Charles Simeon, remember whose you are, and whom you
serve." ' And then the worthy man, in his own inimitable way,

would bow respectfully and say, 'I will not trifle. I will not trifle. I will not forget.'

May we, in conclusion, look to a far higher pattern than any man — Martyn, M'Cheyne, or any other. May we look to the great Chief Shepherd, the great pattern, in whose steps we are to walk! May we abide in him, and never trifle! May we hold on our way, looking to Jesus, keeping clear of the world, its pleasures and its follies, caring nothing for the world's frowns and not much moved by the world's smiles, looking forward to that day when the Great Shepherd will give to all who have done his work and preached his gospel a crown of glory that does not fade away! The more we have the mind of Christ, the more we shall understand what it is to 'give ourselves entirely to these things'.

4.
Pharisees and Sadducees

'Then Jesus said to them, "Take heed and beware of the leaven of the Pharisees and the Sadducees" ' (Matt. 16:6).

Every word spoken by the Lord Jesus is full of deep instruction for Christians. It is the voice of the Chief Shepherd. It is the great Head of the church speaking to all its members, the King of kings speaking to his subjects, the Master of the house speaking to his servants, the Captain of our salvation speaking to his soldiers. Above all, it is the voice of the one who said, 'I have not spoken on my own authority; but the Father who sent me gave me a command, what I should say and what I should speak' (John 12:49). The heart of every believer in the Lord Jesus ought to burn within him when he hears his Master's words; he ought to say, 'This is "the voice of my beloved!" ' (S. of S. 2:8).

And every kind of word spoken by the Lord Jesus is of the greatest value. All his words of doctrine and instruction are as precious as gold; all his parables and prophecies are precious; all his words of comfort and of consolation are precious; last but by no means least, all his words of caution and of warning are precious. We are not merely to hear him when he says, 'Come to me, all you who labour and are heavy laden'; we are also to hear him when he says, 'Take heed and beware...'

I am going to direct your attention to one of the most solemn and emphatic warnings which the Lord Jesus ever delivered: 'Take heed and beware of the leaven of the Pharisees and the Sadducees.' On this text I wish to erect a beacon for all who desire to be saved, and to preserve some souls, if possible, from making shipwreck of their lives. The times call loudly for such beacons; spiritual shipwrecks have been deplorably numerous of late. The watchmen of the church ought to speak out plainly now, or for ever hold their peace.

1. Those to whom the warning was addressed

First of all, I ask my readers to observe who the men were to whom the warning of the text was addressed. Our Lord Jesus Christ was not speaking to men who were worldly, ungodly and unsanctified, but to his own disciples, companions and friends. He addressed men of whom we can say, with the exception of the apostate Judas Iscariot, that their hearts were right in the sight of God. He spoke to the twelve apostles, the first founders of the church of Christ and the first ministers of the word of salvation. And yet even to them he addressed the solemn caution of our text: 'Take heed and beware…'

There is something very remarkable in this fact. We might have thought that these apostles needed little warning of this kind. Had they not given up all for Christ's sake? They had. Had they not endured hardship for Christ's sake? They had. Had they not believed Jesus, followed Jesus, loved Jesus, when almost all the world was unbelieving? All these things are true, and yet to them the caution was addressed: 'Take heed and beware…' We might have imagined that at any rate the disciples had little to fear from the 'leaven of the Pharisees and the Sadducees'. They were poor and uneducated men, most of them fishermen or tax collectors. They were not inclined to be disposed favourably towards the Pharisees and the Sadducees; they were more likely to be prejudiced against them than to feel any drawing towards them. All this is perfectly true; yet even to them there comes the solemn warning: 'Take heed and beware...'

There is useful instruction here for all who claim to love the Lord Jesus Christ in sincerity. It tells us loudly that the most eminent servants of Christ are not beyond the need of warnings, and ought always to be on their guard. It shows us plainly that the holiest of believers ought to walk humbly with his God, and to watch and pray that he may not fall into temptation and be overtaken in some trespass (Gal. 6:1). None is so holy that he is not at risk of falling — not finally and irrevocably, so that he is beyond hope of recovery, but so as to bring disgrace and embarrassment on himself, cause a scandal in the church and give the world occasion to gloat; none is so strong that there is no risk of his being overcome for a time. Chosen as believers are by God the Father, justified as they are by the blood and righteousness of Jesus Christ, sanctified as they are by the Holy Spirit — still believers are only men; they are still in the body and still in the world. They are always close to temptation; they are always liable to make mistakes, both in doctrine and in practice. Their hearts, though renewed, are very weak; their understanding, though enlightened, is still very dim. They ought to live like those who reside in the land of an enemy, and to put on the armour of God every day. The devil is very busy; he never slumbers or sleeps. Let us remember how Noah, Abraham, Lot, Moses, David and Peter all fell and, remembering them, be humble and take care that we too do not fall.

I may be allowed to say that none need warnings so much as the ministers of Christ's gospel. Our office and our ordination are no security against errors and mistakes. It is, sadly, only too true that the greatest heresies have crept into the church of Christ by means of ordained men. Ordination, whether by a bishop, or by elders, or whatever other form it may take, does not confer any immunity from error and false doctrine. Our very familiarity with the gospel often creates in us a hardened state of mind. We are apt to read the Scriptures and preach the Word and conduct public worship and carry on the service of God in a dry, hard, formal, callous spirit. Our very familiarity with sacred things is likely to lead us astray if we do not carefully watch our hearts. 'Nowhere,' says an old writer, 'is a man's soul in more danger than in the ministerial office.'

The history of the church of Christ contains many dismal proofs that the most distinguished ministers may for a time fall away. Who has not heard of Archbishop Cranmer recanting and going back from those opinions he had defended so stoutly — though, by God's mercy, he was raised again to witness a glorious confession at last? Or there was Bishop Jewell, who signed documents that he most thoroughly disapproved and afterwards bitterly repented signing them. Who does not know that many others might be named who, at one time or another, have been overtaken by trespasses, have fallen into errors and been led astray? And who does not know the mournful fact that many of them never came back to the truth, but died in hardness of heart, and held their errors to the end?

These things ought to make us humble and cautious. They tell us to distrust our own hearts and to pray to be kept from falling. In these days, when we are especially called upon to hold firmly to the doctrines of the Protestant Reformation, let us be on our guard that our devotion to the cause of Protestantism does not make us proud and conceited. Let us never say boastfully, 'I shall never fall into the errors of Roman Catholicism or liberalism: those views will never suit me.' Let us remember that many have begun well and run well for a time, and yet afterwards turned aside out of the right way. Let us take care to see that we are spiritual men as well as Protestants, and real friends of Christ as well as enemies of Antichrist. Let us pray that we may be kept from error, and never

forget that the twelve apostles themselves were the men to
whom the great Head of the church addressed these words:
'Take heed and beware...'

2. The dangers against which the Lord warned the apostles

I propose, in the second place, to explain what those dangers
were against which our Lord warned the apostles. 'Take heed,'
he says, 'and beware of the leaven of the Pharisees and the
Sadducees.'

The danger against which he warns them is *false doctrine*.
He says nothing about the sword of persecution, or the open
breach of the Ten Commandments, or the love of money, or
the love of pleasure. All these things no doubt were dangers
and snares to which the souls of the apostles were exposed,
but against these things our Lord raises no warning voice here.
His warning is confined to one single point: 'the leaven of the
Pharisees and of the Sadducees'. We are not left to conjecture
what our Lord meant by that word 'leaven'. Just a few verses
after this very text to which I am drawing your attention, the
Holy Spirit tells us plainly that by 'leaven' he meant the 'doctrine' of the Pharisees and Sadducees (Matt. 16:12).

Let us try to understand what we mean when we speak of
the 'doctrine of the Pharisees and Sadducees'.

The Pharisees

The doctrine of the Pharisees may be summed up in three
words: they were *formalists, tradition-worshippers* and *self-
righteous*. They attached such weight to the traditions of men
that they practically regarded them as of more importance than
the inspired writings of the Old Testament. They prided themselves on their excessive strictness in attending to all the

ceremonial requirements of the law of Moses. They thought
much of being descended from Abraham, and said in their
hearts, 'We have Abraham as our father.' They imagined that
because they had Abraham as their father they were not in
danger of hell like other men, and that their descent from him
somehow entitled them to heaven. They attached great value
to washings and ceremonial purification of the body, and believed that the very act of touching the dead body of a fly or a
gnat would defile them. They made a great fuss about the outward aspects of religion, and such things as could be seen by
men. They made their phylacteries broad and enlarged the
fringes of their garments. They prided themselves on paying
great honour to dead saints and ornamenting the graves of the
righteous. They were very zealous to make converts. They
thought much of having power, rank and pre-eminence and of
being called 'Rabbi, Rabbi,' by men. These things, and many
similar things, the Pharisees did. Every well-informed Christian can find these things in the Gospels of Matthew and Mark
(see Matt. 15; 23; Mark 7).

All this time, we need to remember, they did not formally
deny any part of the Old Testament Scripture. But they brought
in, over and above it, so much of human invention that they
virtually put Scripture aside and buried it under their own traditions. This is the sort of religion, of which our Lord says to
the apostles, 'Take heed and beware...'

The Sadducees

The doctrine of the Sadducees, on the other hand, may be
summed up in these three words: *free-thinking, scepticism* and
rationalism. Their creed was far less popular than that of the
Pharisees and, therefore, we find them mentioned less often in
the New Testament Scriptures. So far as we can judge from
the New Testament, they appear to have held the doctrine of

varying degrees of inspiration; at any rate they attached a far higher value to the Pentateuch [the first five books of the Old Testament] than to all the other parts of the Old Testament if, indeed, they did not altogether ignore the latter. They believed that there was no resurrection, and that there were no angels or spirits, and they tried to laugh men out of their belief in these things by bringing forward difficult questions. We have an instance of their mode of argument in the case which they propounded to our Lord of the woman who had had seven husbands, when they asked, 'In the resurrection, whose wife of the seven will she be?' And in this way they probably hoped, by rendering religion absurd, and its chief doctrines ridiculous, to make men altogether give up the faith they had received from the Scriptures.

All this time, we need to remember, we cannot say that the Sadducees were downright unbelievers; they were not. We may not say they denied revelation altogether; they did not do this. They observed the law of Moses. Many of them were found among the priests in the times described in the Acts of the Apostles. Caiaphas, who condemned our Lord, was a Sadducee. But the practical effect of their teaching was to shake men's faith in any revelation and to throw a cloud of doubt over men's minds, which was only one degree better than unbelief. And of all such kind of doctrine — free-thinking, scepticism, rationalism — our Lord says, 'Take heed and beware...'

Why did the Lord deliver this warning?

Now the question arises, why did our Lord Jesus Christ deliver this warning? He knew, no doubt, that within forty years the schools of the Pharisees and the Sadducees would be completely overthrown. He, who knew all things from the beginning, knew perfectly well that in forty years Jerusalem, with its magnificent temple, would be destroyed and the Jews scattered over the face of the earth. Why, then, do we find him giving this warning about 'the leaven of the Pharisees and Sadducees'?

I believe that our Lord delivered this solemn warning for the perpetual benefit of the church which he came to earth to found. He spoke with a prophetic knowledge. He well knew the diseases to which human nature is always liable. He foresaw that the two great plagues of his church on earth would always be the doctrine of the Pharisees and the doctrine of the Sadducees. He knew that these would act like two huge millstones, between which his truth would be perpetually crushed and ground until he came the second time. He knew that among professing Christians there would always be those who were Pharisees in spirit and those who were Sadducees in spirit. He knew that they would never fail to have successors and their generation would never become extinct, and that though the names of Pharisees and Sadducees no longer existed, yet the principles which they represented would always exist. He knew that during the time that the church existed, until his return, there would always be some that would add to the Word and some that would subtract from it, some that would smother it by adding other things to it, and some that would bleed it to death by subtracting from its principal truths. And this is the reason why we find him delivering this solemn warning: 'Take heed and beware of the leaven of the Pharisees and the Sadducees.'

And now comes the question, did not our Lord Jesus Christ have good reason to give this warning? I appeal to all who know anything of church history — was there not indeed a cause? I appeal to all who remember what took place soon after the apostles were dead. Do we not read that in the early days of the church of Christ there rose up two distinct parties:

one ever inclined to err, like the Arians [who denied the divinity of Christ], in holding less than the truth; the other ever inclined to err, like the worshippers of relics and saints, in holding more than the truth as it is in Jesus? Do we not see the same thing coming out in later times, in the form of Roman Catholicism on the one side and Socinianism [the elevation of the human reason and denial of basic doctrines such as the Trinity, the Fall and the atonement] on the other? These are ancient things. Space does not permit me to enter more fully into them here. They are things well known to all who are familiar with records of past days. There always have been these two great parties: the party representing the principles of the Pharisee, and the party representing the principles of the Sadducee. And therefore our Lord had good cause to say of these two great principles, 'Take heed and beware...'

But I desire to bring the subject even closer home at the present moment. I ask my readers to consider whether warnings like this are not especially needed in our own times? We have, undoubtedly, much to be thankful for in this land. We have made great advances in arts and sciences in the last few centuries, and have much of the outward form and appearance of morality and religion. But, I ask anybody who can see beyond his own front door, or his own fireside, whether we do not live in the midst of dangers from false doctrine?

We have among us, on the one side, a group of men who, wittingly or unwittingly, are paving the way to return to the church of Rome — a party that professes to draw its principles from primitive tradition, the writings of the Fathers and the voice of the church; a party that talks and writes so much about the church, the ministry and the sacraments that it makes them, like Aaron's rod, swallow up everything else in Christianity; a party that attaches vast importance to the outward form and ceremonial of religion, to gestures, postures, ritual bowing, the use of crosses, holy water, special chancel seats for the clergy, side-tables to hold the sacrament, elaborate carved screens, vestments, altar cloths, incense, statues, banners, processions, floral decorations, and many other similar things, about which not a word is to be found in the Holy Scriptures as having any place in Christian worship. I refer, of course, to the school of clergymen called Ritualists. When we examine the proceedings of that school, there can be only one conclusion concerning them. Whatever the meaning and intention of their teachers may be, however devoted, zealous and self-denying many of them are, I believe that it is on them that the mantle of the Pharisees has fallen.

We have, on the other hand, a party of men who, wittingly or unwittingly, appear to pave the way to denial of the fundamental doctrines of Christianity — a school of thought which holds strange views about the entire and unqualified inspiration of Holy Scripture, even more strange views about the doctrine of sacrifice and the atonement of our Lord and Saviour Jesus Christ, strange views about the eternity of punishment and God's love to man; a school strong in negatives but very weak in positives, skilful in raising doubts but powerless to remove them, clever in unsettling men's faith and loosening its hold on truth, but powerless to offer any firm ground for the soles of our feet to tread on. And, whether the leaders of this party mean it or not, I believe that on them has fallen the mantle of the Sadducees.

These things sound harsh. It saves a vast deal of trouble to shut our eyes and say, 'I see no danger,' and because it is not seen, therefore not to believe it. It is easy to put plugs in our ears and say, 'I hear nothing,' and because we hear nothing therefore to feel no alarm. But we are well aware who are the ones who rejoice over the state of things we have to deplore in some quarters of the Anglican Church. We know what the

Roman Catholic thinks; we know what the liberal thinks. The Roman Catholic rejoices over the rise of Anglo-Catholicism: the liberal rejoices over the rise of men who teach such views as those set forth in modern days about the atonement and inspiration. They would not rejoice as they do if they did not see their work being done and their cause being helped forward. The danger, I believe, is far greater than we are apt to suppose. The books that are read in many quarters are liable to do considerable harm and the tone of thought on religious subjects among many classes of people is deeply unsatisfactory. The plague is at large. If we love life, we ought to search our own hearts and test our own faith, and make sure that we stand on the right foundation. Above all, we ought to take heed that we ourselves do not absorb any of the poison of false doctrine, and go back from our first love.

I feel deeply the painfulness of speaking out on these subjects. I am well aware that plain-speaking about false doctrine is very unpopular and that the speaker must be willing to find himself being thought of as very uncharitable, very troublesome and very narrow-minded. Thousands of people can never distinguish differences in religion. To the bulk of men a clergyman is a clergyman, and a sermon is a sermon and, as to any difference between one minister and another, or one doctrine and another, they are utterly unable to understand it. I cannot expect such people to approve of any warning against false doctrine. I must make up my mind to meet with their disapproval and must bear it as best I can.

But I will ask any honest-minded, unprejudiced Bible reader to turn to the New Testament and see what he will find there. He will find many plain warnings against false doctrine: 'Beware of false prophets' (Matt. 7:15). 'Beware lest anyone cheat you through philosophy and empty deceit' (Col. 2:8). 'Do not be carried about with various and strange doctrines' (Heb.

13:9). 'Do not believe every spirit, but test the spirits, whether they are of God' (1 John 4:1). He will find a large part of several inspired epistles taken up with elaborate explanations of true doctrine and warnings against false teaching. I ask whether it is possible for a minister who takes the Bible for his rule of faith to avoid giving warnings against doctrinal error?

Finally, I ask anyone to take note what is going on in England. I ask whether it is not true that hundreds have left the Established Church and joined the church of Rome? I ask whether it is not true that hundreds remain within the Anglican Church, who in heart are little better than Roman Catholics and who ought, if they are consistent, to walk in the steps of Newman[1] and others who have left, and go to the church where they belong? I ask again whether it is not true that young men by the score, both at Oxford and Cambridge, are spoiled and ruined by the withering influence of scepticism, and have lost all positive principles in religion? Sneers at religious newspapers, loud declarations of dislike of being associated with a particular party, high-sounding, vague phrases about 'deep thinking, broad views, new light, free handling of Scripture, and the weakness and ineffectiveness of certain schools of theology' make up the whole Christianity of many of the rising generation. And yet, in the face of these well-known facts, men cry out, 'Hold your peace about false doctrine. Leave false doctrine alone!' I cannot hold my peace. Faith in the Word of God, love to the souls of men, the vows I took when I was ordained, alike compel me to bear witness against the errors of the day. And I believe that this saying of our Lord is eminently a truth for the times: 'Beware of the leaven of the Pharisees and the Sadducees.'

---

1. One of the founders of the Oxford Movement, which led to the rise of Anglo-Catholicism in the Church of England. He eventually left the Church of England and joined the Roman Catholic Church, becoming a cardinal. A number of his hymns are still widely sung today.

3. The name by which the Lord describes these false doctrines

The third thing to which I wish to call attention is the strange name by which our Lord Jesus Christ speaks of the doctrines of the Pharisees and of the Sadducees.

The words which our Lord used were always the wisest and the best that could be used. He might have said, 'Take heed and beware of the doctrine', or of 'the teaching', or of 'the opinions of the Pharisees and the Sadducees.' But he does not say so. He uses a word that strikes us as strange. He says, 'Take heed and beware of the leaven of the Pharisees and the Sadducees.'

Now I am sure we all know what is the true meaning of the word 'leaven'. It is what we commonly call 'yeast' — the yeast which is added to the lump of dough in making a loaf of bread. This yeast, or leaven, is only very small in proportion to the lump into which it is thrown; in the same way, our Lord would have us know, the first beginning of false doctrine is only small compared to the whole body of Christianity. It works quietly and noiselessly; in the same way, our Lord would have us know, false doctrine works secretly in the heart in which it is once planted. It insensibly changes the character of the whole mass with which it is mixed; in the same way, our Lord would have us know, the doctrines of the Pharisees and Sadducees turn everything upside down, when they are once admitted into a church or into a man's heart. Let us take note of these points; they throw light on many things that we see in the present day. It is of vast importance to receive the lessons of wisdom that this word 'leaven' contains in itself.

False doctrine does not meet men face to face, and proclaim that it is false. It does not blow a trumpet before it and endeavour openly to turn us away from the truth as it is in Jesus. It does not come before men in broad daylight, and summon them to surrender. It approaches us secretly, quietly, insidiously, plausibly, and in such a way as to disarm man's suspicion and throw him off his guard. It is the wolf in sheep's clothing and Satan in the garb of an angel of light who have always proved the most dangerous enemies of the church of Christ.

I believe the most powerful champion of the Pharisees is not the man who invites you openly and honestly to come out and join the church of Rome; it is the man who says that he agrees on all points with you in *doctrine*. He would not take anything away from those evangelical views that you hold; indeed, he would not have you make any changes at all. All he asks you to do is to *add* a little more to your belief, in order to make your Christianity perfect. 'Believe me,' he says, 'we do not want you to give up anything. We only want you to hold a few more clear views about the church and the sacraments. We want you to add to your present opinions a little more about the office of the ministry, and a little more about the authority of bishops, and a little more about the Prayer Book and a little more about the necessity of order and of discipline. We only want you to add *a little more* of these things to your system of religion, and you will be quite right.' But when men speak to you in this way, then is the time to remember what our Lord said and to 'take heed and beware…' This is the leaven of the Pharisees, against which we are to stand on our guard.

Why do I say this? I say it because there is no security against the doctrine of the Pharisees, unless we resist its principles in their early stages. Beginning with a 'little more about the church', you may one day end up putting the church in the place of Christ. Beginning with a 'little more about the ministry', you may one day come to regard the minister as 'the mediator between God and man'. Beginning with a 'little more about the sacraments', you may end up one day by altogether giving up the doctrine of justification by faith without the deeds of the law. Beginning with a 'little more reverence for the Prayer Book', you may one day come to place it above the holy Word of God himself. Beginning with a 'little more honour to bishops', you may at last refuse salvation to everyone who does not belong to a church which recognizes the office of bishop. I am only telling an old story; I am only marking out roads that have been trodden by hundreds of members of the Church of England over the years. They began by finding fault with the Reformers, and have ended by swallowing the decrees of the Council of Trent.[2] They began by praising Archbishop Laud and those who refused to take the oath of allegiance to Protestantism in the days of William and Mary and have ended by going far beyond them and formally joining the church of Rome. I believe that when we hear men asking us to 'add a little more' to our good old, plain, evangelical views, we should stand on our guard. We should remember our Lord's caution: 'Take heed and beware of the leaven of the Pharisees.'

I consider the most dangerous champion of the school of the Sadducees is not the man who tells you openly that he wants you to lay aside any part of the truth and to become a free-thinker and a sceptic. It is the man who begins with quietly insinuating doubts as to the position that we ought to take up about religion — doubts whether we ought to be so positive in saying, 'This is truth, and that falsehood'; doubts whether we ought to think men wrong who differ from us on religious opinions, since they may, after all, be as much right as we are. It is the man who tells us we ought not to condemn anybody's views, lest we err on the side of being uncharitable. It is the man who always begins talking in a vague way about God being a God of love and hints that we ought to believe perhaps

---

2. i.e. the doctrines of the Roman Catholic Church. The Council of Trent was an assembly of church leaders convened between the years 1545 and 1563 in response to the spread of the Reformation in Europe. It clarified and redefined the official position of the Roman Catholic Church on a number of key doctrines.

that all men, whatever doctrine they profess, will be saved. It
is the man who is always reminding us that we ought to take
care how we think lightly of men of powerful minds and great
intellects who do not think as we do (even though they are
deists and sceptics), and who tells us that, after all, 'Great
minds are all, more or less, taught of God!' It is the man who
is constantly harping on the difficulties of inspiration and raising questions whether all men may not be found to be saved in
the end, and whether all may not be right in the sight of God.
It is the man who crowns this kind of talk by a few calm sneers
against what he is pleased to call 'old-fashioned views' and
'narrow-minded theology' and 'bigotry' and the lack of 'tolerance and love' in the present day. But when men begin to
speak to us in this kind of way, then is the time to stand on our
guard. Then is the time to remember the words of our Lord
Jesus Christ and to 'take heed and beware of the leaven of ...
the Sadducees'.

Once more, why do I say this? I say it because there is no
security against the doctrine of the Sadducees, any more than
there is against that of the Pharisees, unless we resist its principles in the bud. Beginning with a little vague talk about 'love',
you may end in the doctrine of universal salvation, fill heaven
with a mixed multitude of wicked as well as good and deny
the existence of hell. Beginning with a few high-sounding
phrases about intellect and the inner light in man, you may end
with denying the work of the Holy Spirit and maintaining that
Homer and Shakespeare were as truly inspired as Paul and
thus practically casting the Bible aside. Beginning with some
dreamy, misty idea about 'all religions containing more or less
truth', you may end with utterly denying the necessity of
missions, and maintaining that the best plan is to leave everybody alone. Beginning with dislike to 'evangelical religion',
as old-fashioned, narrow and exclusive, you may end by re-
jecting every leading doctrine of Christianity — the atone-

ment, the need of grace and the divinity of Christ. Again I repeat that I am only telling an old story; I am only giving a sketch of a path which great numbers have trodden over the years. They were once satisfied with such theology as that of Newton, Scott, Cecil and Romaine; they are now fancying they have found a more excellent way in the principles which have been propounded by theologians of the liberal school! I believe there is no safety for a man's soul unless he remembers the lesson involved in those solemn words: 'Beware of the leaven of the ... Sadducees.'

Let us beware of *the insidious nature* of false doctrine. Like the fruit of which Eve and Adam ate, it looks at first sight pleasant and good and a thing to be desired. It is not labelled 'poison' and so people are not afraid. Like a counterfeit coin, it is not stamped with the message 'bad'; it passes for the real thing because of the very likeness it bears to the truth.

Let us beware of the *very small beginnings* of false doctrine. Every heresy began at one time with some little departure from the truth. There is only a little seed of error needed to create a great tree. It is the little stones that make up the mighty building. It was the little timbers that made the great ark that carried Noah and his family over a submerged world at the time of the flood. It is the little leaven that leavens the whole lump. It is the little flaw in one link of the chain cable that wrecks the gallant ship and drowns the crew. It is the omission or addition of one little item in the doctor's prescription that spoils the whole medicine and turns it into poison. We do not tolerate quietly a little dishonesty, or a little cheating, or a little lying; in the same way, let us never allow a little false doctrine to ruin us, by thinking it is only 'a little one' and can do no harm. The Galatians seemed to be doing nothing very dangerous when they were observing 'days and months and seasons and years', yet Paul says, 'I am afraid for you' (Gal. 4:10,11).

Finally, let us beware of *supposing that we at any rate are not in danger.* 'Our views are sound. Our feet stand firm. Others may fall away, but we are safe!' Hundreds have thought the same, and have come to a bad end. In their self-confidence they tampered with little temptations and little forms of false doctrine; in their self-conceit they went near the brink of danger; and now they seem lost for ever. They appear given over to a strong delusion, so as to believe a lie. Some of them have exchanged the Prayer Book for the Roman Catholic breviary and are praying to the Virgin Mary and bowing down to images. Others of them are casting overboard one doctrine after another, and appear likely to strip themselves of every sort of religion apart from a few scraps of Deism. Very striking is the imagery in *Pilgrim's Progress* which describes the hill Error as 'very steep on the farthest side', and says that 'When Christian and Hopeful looked down they saw at the bottom several men dashed all to pieces by a fall they had from the top.' Never, never let us forget the caution to beware of 'leaven', and if we think we stand, let us 'take heed that we do not fall'.

4. Some safeguards and remedies

I propose in the fourth and last place, to suggest some safeguards against and antidotes to the dangers of the present day, which we have described as the leaven of the Pharisees and the leaven of the Sadducees.

I feel that we all need more and more the presence of the Holy Spirit in our hearts to guide, to teach and to keep us sound in the faith. We all need to watch more and to pray to be sustained and preserved from falling away. But still, there are certain great truths which we are specially bound to keep in mind. There are times when some common epidemic invades a land, when medicines that are valuable at all times become of special value. There are places where a particular strain of malaria is prevalent, in which remedies that are valuable in every place are more valuable than ever as a consequence of the presence of this disease. So I believe there are times and seasons in the church of Christ when we are bound to tighten our hold upon certain great leading truths, to grasp them with more than ordinary firmness in our hands, to press them to our hearts and not to let them go. I desire to set such doctrines forth in order as the great antidotes to the poisonous leaven of the Pharisees and the Sadducees. When Saul and Jonathan were killed by the archers, David ordered the Israelites to be taught the use of the bow.

The total corruption of human nature

For one thing, if we would be kept sound in the faith, we must keep a careful watch on our doctrine about the total corruption of human nature. The corruption of human nature is no slight thing. It is no partial, skin-deep disease, but a radical and universal corruption of man's will, intellect, affections and conscience. We are not merely poor, pitiful sinners in God's sight: we are guilty sinners; we are blameworthy sinners; we deserve justly God's wrath and God's condemnation. I believe there are very few errors and false doctrines the beginning of which may not be traced up to faulty views about the corruption of human nature. Wrong views of a disease will always bring with them wrong views of the remedy. Wrong views of the corruption of human nature will always carry with them wrong views of the grand antidote to, and cure of, that corruption.

The inspiration and authority of Scripture

For another thing, we must keep a very careful watch on our doctrine about the inspiration and authority of the Holy Scriptures. Let us boldly maintain, in the face of all who say the contrary, that the whole of the Bible is given by inspiration of the Holy Spirit, that all is inspired completely — not one part more than another — and that there is an entire gulf between the Word of God and any other book in the world.

We need not be afraid of difficulties in the way of the doctrine of entire and unqualified inspiration.[3] There may be many things about it far too high for us to comprehend; it is a miracle, and all miracles are necessarily mysterious. But if we are not to believe anything until we can entirely explain it, there are very few things indeed that we shall believe.

We need not be afraid of all the assaults that criticism brings to bear upon the Bible. From the days of the apostles the Word of the Lord has been incessantly 'tried', and has never failed to come forth as gold, uninjured and untarnished.

We need not be afraid of the discoveries of science. Astronomers may sweep the heavens with telescopes and geologists may dig down into the heart of the earth and never shake the authority of the Bible: 'The voice of God and the work of God's hands never will be found to contradict one another.'

We need not be afraid of the researches of travellers. They will never discover anything that contradicts God's Bible. I believe that if an archaeologist were to go over all the earth and dig up a hundred buried Ninevehs, there would not be found a single inscription which would contradict a single fact in the Word of God.

We must also boldly maintain that this Word of God is the only rule of faith and of practice, that anything that is not written in it cannot be required of any man as necessary for salvation, and that however plausibly new doctrines may be defended, if they are not found in the Word of God they cannot be worth our attention. It does not matter in the least who says a thing — whether he is a bishop, archdeacon, dean, or

---

3. The technical term used by Ryle is 'plenary inspiration'.

presbyter. It does not matter that the thing is well expressed, said eloquently, attractively, forcibly, and in such a way as to turn the laugh against you. We are not to believe it unless it is proved to us by Holy Scripture.

Last, but not least, we must use the Bible as if we believed it was given by inspiration. We must use it with reverence, and read it with all the tenderness with which we would read the words of an absent father. We must not expect to find no mysteries in a book inspired by the Spirit of God. We must rather remember that in nature there are many things we cannot understand, and that, as it is in the book of nature, so it will always be in the book of revelation. We should draw near to the Word of God in that spirit of reverence recommended by Lord Bacon many years ago. 'Remember,' he says, speaking of the book of nature, 'that man is not the master of that book, but the interpreter of that book.' And in the same way as we deal with the book of nature, so we must deal with the book of God. We must draw near to it, not to teach, but to learn; not like the master of it but like a humble pupil, seeking to understand it.

The atonement and sacrificial work of Christ

For another thing, we must keep a careful watch on our doctrine with regard to the atonement and priestly office of our Lord and Saviour Jesus Christ. We must boldly maintain that the death of our Lord on the cross was no common death. It was not the death of one who only died as a martyr, like Cranmer, Ridley and Latimer. It was not the death of one who only died to give us a mighty example of self-sacrifice and self-denial. The death of Christ was an offering up to God of Christ's own body and blood, to make satisfaction for man's sin and violation of God's law. It was a sacrifice and propitiation — a sacrifice represented in symbolic form in every offering of the law of Moses, a sacrifice of the mightiest influence on all mankind. Without the shedding of that blood there could not be, there never was to be, any remission of sin.

In addition, we must boldly maintain that this crucified Saviour is seated for ever at the right hand of God to make intercession for all who come to God by him, that he there represents and pleads for those who put their trust in him, and that he has delegated his office of Priest and Mediator to no one, or to no group of men, on the face of the earth. We need no one else. We need no Virgin Mary, no angels, no saints, no priests, no person, ordained or unordained, to stand between us and God, other than the one Mediator, Christ Jesus.

We must also boldly maintain that peace of conscience is not to be bought by confession to a priest, and by receiving a man's absolution from sin. It is to be had only by going to the great High Priest, Christ Jesus, by confession before him, not before man, and only by absolution from him who alone can say, 'Your sins are forgiven. Go in peace.'

Last, but not least, we must boldly maintain that peace with God, once obtained by faith in Christ, is to be kept up, not by mere outward ceremonial acts of worship, not by receiving the sacrament of the Lord's Supper every day; but by the daily habit of looking to the Lord Jesus Christ by faith, eating by faith his body and drinking by faith his blood — that eating and drinking of which our Lord says that he who eats and drinks shall find his flesh to be 'food indeed', and his blood to be 'drink indeed' (John 6:55). The saintly John Owen declared, long ago, that if there was any one point more than another that Satan wished to overthrow, it was the priestly office of our Lord and Saviour Jesus Christ. Satan well knew, he said, that it was the 'principal foundation of faith and consolation of the church'. Right views about that office are of essential importance in the present day, if men would not fall into error.

The work of the Holy Spirit

One more remedy I must mention. We must keep a careful watch on our doctrine about the work of God the Holy Spirit. Let us settle it in our minds that his work is no uncertain, invisible operation on the heart, and that where he is, he is not hidden, not unfelt, not unobserved. We do not believe that the dew, when it falls, cannot be felt, or that where there is life in a man it cannot be seen and observed by his breath. So is it with the influence of the Holy Spirit. No one has any right to lay claim to it, unless its fruits, its known and felt effects, can be seen in his life. Where he is, there will always be a new creation and a new man. Where he is, there will always be new knowledge, new faith, new holiness, new fruits in the life, in the family, in the world, in the church. And where these new things are not to be seen we may well say with confidence that there is no work of the Holy Spirit. These are times in which we all need to be on our guard about the doctrine of the work of the Spirit. Madame Guyon said, long ago, that the time would perhaps come when men might have to be martyrs for the work of the Holy Spirit. That time seems not far distant. At any rate, if there is one truth in religion that seems to have more contempt showered upon it than another, it is the work of the Spirit.

I desire to impress the immense importance of these four points upon all who read this book:

1. clear views of the sinfulness of human nature;
2. clear views of the inspiration of Scripture;
3. clear views of the atonement and priestly office of our Lord and Saviour Jesus Christ;
4. clear views of the work of the Holy Spirit.

I believe that strange doctrines about the church, the ministry and the sacraments, about the love of God, the death of Christ and the eternity of punishment, will find no foothold in the heart which is sound on these four points. I believe that they are four great safeguards against the leaven of the Pharisees and the Sadducees.

What this means for each of us

I will now conclude this chapter with a few remarks by way of practical application. My desire is to make the whole subject useful to those into whose hands these pages may fall, and to supply an answer to the questions which may possibly arise in some hearts: 'What are we to do? What advice have you got to offer for these times?'

In the first place, I will ask every reader of this book to *find out whether he has saving personal religion for his own soul.* This is the principal thing, after all. It will profit no one to belong to the membership of a sound church, if he does not himself belong to Christ. It will be of no use to a man to be intellectually sound in the faith, and to approve sound doctrine, if he is not himself sound at heart. Is this the case with you? Can you say that your heart is right in the sight of God? Is it renewed by the Holy Spirit? Does Christ dwell in it by faith? Oh, do not rest, do not rest till you can give a satisfactory answer to these questions! The man who dies unconverted, however sound his views, is as truly lost for ever as the worst Pharisee or Sadducee that ever lived.

In the next place, let me entreat every reader who desires to be sound in the faith to *study the Bible diligently.* That blessed book is given to be a light to our feet, and a lamp to our path. No one who reads it reverently, prayerfully, humbly and regularly shall ever be allowed to miss the way to heaven.

By it every sermon and every religious book and every ministry ought to be weighed and proved. Would you know what is
truth? Do you feel confused and puzzled by the war of words
which you hear on every side about religion? Do you want to
know what you ought to believe, and what you ought to be
and do in order to be saved? Take down your Bible, and stop
listening to man. Read your Bible with earnest prayer for the
teaching of the Holy Spirit; read it with honest determination
to abide by its lessons. Do so steadily and perseveringly, and
you will see light: you will be kept from the leaven of the
Pharisees and Sadducees and be guided to eternal life. The
way to do a thing is to do it. Act upon this advice without
delay.

In the next place, let me advise every reader who has reason to hope that he is sound in faith and heart to *take care to
give each truth its rightful place.* I mean by that to impress on
you the importance of giving each individual truth of Christianity the same place and position in our hearts which is given
to it in God's Word. The first things must not be put second,
and the second things must not be put first in our religion. The
church must not be put above Christ. The sacraments must
not be put above faith and the work of the Holy Spirit. Ministers must not be exalted above the place assigned to them by
Christ; means of grace must not be regarded as an end instead
of a means. Attention to this point is of great importance; the
mistakes which arise from neglecting it are neither few nor
small. Here lies the immense importance of studying the whole
Word of God, omitting nothing and avoiding partiality in reading one part more than another. Here again lies the value of
having a clear system of Christianity in our minds. It would be
well for the Church of England if all its members read the
Thirty-Nine Articles and took note of the beautiful order in
which those articles state the main truths which men ought to
believe.

In the next place, let me entreat every true-hearted servant of Christ not to be deceived by the apparently harmless disguise under which false doctrines often approach our souls in the present day. Beware of supposing that a teacher of religion is to be trusted because, although he holds some unsound views, yet he 'teaches a great deal of truth'. Such a teacher is precisely the man to do you harm; poison is always most dangerous when it is given in small doses and mixed with wholesome food. Beware of being taken in by the apparent earnestness of many of the teachers and proponents of false doctrine. Remember that zeal, sincerity and fervour are no proof whatever that a man is working for Christ, and ought to be believed. Peter no doubt was in earnest when he told our Lord to spare himself, and not go to the cross; yet our Lord said to him, 'Get behind me, Satan!' Saul no doubt was in earnest when he went to and fro persecuting Christians; yet he did it ignorantly, and his zeal was not according to knowledge. The founders of the Spanish Inquisition no doubt were in earnest, and in burning God's saints alive thought they were doing God service; yet they were actually persecuting Christ's members and walking in the steps of Cain. It is an awful fact that 'Satan himself transforms himself into an angel of light' (2 Cor. 11:14). Of all the delusions prevalent in these latter days, there is none greater than the common notion that 'If a man is in earnest about his religion he must be a good man!' Beware of being carried away by this delusion; beware of being led astray by men just because they are in earnest about a particular doctrine. Being in earnest is in itself an excellent thing, but it must be earnestness on behalf of Christ and his whole truth, or else it is worth nothing at all. The things that are highly esteemed among men are often abominable in the sight of God.

In the next place, let me counsel every true servant of Christ to *examine his own heart* frequently and carefully as to his state before God. This is a practice which is useful at all times;

it is especially desirable at the present day. When the great plague of London was at its height people took note of the smallest symptoms that appeared on their bodies in a way that they never noticed them before. A spot here, or a spot there, which in time of health men thought nothing of, received close attention when the plague was decimating families and striking down one after another! So it ought to be with us, in the times in which we live. We ought to watch our hearts with double watchfulness. We ought to give more time to meditation, self-examination and reflection. It is a hurrying, bustling age; if we would be kept from falling, we must make time for being frequently alone with God.

Last of all, let me urge all true believers to *contend earnestly for the faith which was once for all delivered to the saints*. We have no cause to be ashamed of that faith. I am firmly persuaded that there is no system so life-giving, so calculated to wake the sleeping, lead on the enquiring and build up the saints as that system which is called the evangelical system of Christianity. Wherever it is faithfully preached and efficiently carried out, and consistently adorned by the lives of those who profess it, it is the power of God. It may be spoken against and mocked by some, but so it was in the days of the apostles. It may be weakly set forth and defended by many of its advocates but, after all, its fruits and its results are its highest praise. No other system of religion can point to such fruits. Nowhere are so many souls converted to God as in those congregations where the gospel of Jesus Christ is preached in all its fulness, without any mixture of the doctrine of the Pharisees or Sadducees. We are not called upon, beyond all doubt, to be nothing but controversialists, but we never ought to be ashamed to testify to the truth as it is in Jesus, and to stand up boldly for evangelical religion. We have the truth, and we need not be afraid to say so. The judgement-day will prove who is right, and to that day we may boldly appeal.

5.
Various and strange doctrines

'Do not be carried about with various and strange doctrines. For it is good that the heart be established by grace, not with foods which have not profited those who have been occupied with them' (Heb. 13:9).

The text which is quoted at the head of this chapter is an apostolic caution against false doctrine. It forms part of a warning which Paul addressed to Hebrew Christians. It is a caution just as much needed now as it was nearly two thousand years ago. Never, I think, was it so important for Christian ministers to cry aloud continually, 'Do not be carried about.'

That old enemy of mankind, the devil, has no more subtle device for ruining souls than that of spreading false doctrine. A murderer and a liar from the beginning, he never stops prowling around, 'seeking whom he may devour'. Outside the church he is constantly persuading men to maintain barbaric customs and destructive superstitions. Human sacrifice to idols, gross, revolting, cruel, disgusting worship of abominable false gods, persecution, slavery, cannibalism, child murder, devastating religious wars — all these are a part of Satan's handiwork and the fruit of his suggestions. Like a pirate, his object is to 'sink, burn and destroy'. Inside the church he is constantly labouring to sow heresies, to propagate errors, to foster departures from the faith. If he cannot prevent the waters flowing from the fountain of life, he tries hard to poison them. If he cannot destroy the healing medicine of the gospel, he strives to adulterate and corrupt it. No wonder that he is called 'Apollyon', the destroyer (Rev. 9:11).

The divine Comforter of the church, the Holy Spirit, has always employed one great agent to oppose Satan's evil schemes. That agent is the Word of God. The Word expounded and unfolded, the Word explained and opened up, the Word made clear to the head and applied to the heart — the Word is the chosen weapon by which the devil must be confronted and confounded. The Word was the sword which the Lord Jesus wielded in the temptation. To every assault of the tempter he replied, 'It is written...' The Word is the sword which his ministers must use in the present day, if they would successfully resist the devil. The Bible, faithfully and freely expounded, is the safeguard of Christ's church.

I desire to remember this lesson, and to invite attention to the text which stands at the head of this paper. We live in an age when men claim to dislike dogmas and creeds and are filled with a morbid dislike of controversial theology. The man who dares to say of one doctrine that 'It is true,' and of another that 'It is false,' must expect to be called narrow-minded and uncharitable and to lose the praise of men. Nevertheless, the Scripture was not written in vain. Let us examine the mighty lessons contained in Paul's words to the Hebrews. They are lessons for us as well as for them.

1. First, we have here a broad warning: 'Do not be carried about with various and strange doctrines.'

2. Secondly, we have here a valuable prescription: 'It is good that the heart be established by grace, not with foods...'

3. Lastly, we have here an instructive fact: 'Foods ... have not profited those who have been occupied with them.'

On each of these points I have something to say. If we patiently plough up this field of truth, we shall find that there is precious treasure hidden in it.

1. A broad warning

First comes the broad warning: 'Do not be carried about with various and strange doctrines.' The meaning of these words is not a hard thing which we cannot understand. 'Do not be tossed to and fro,' the apostle seems to say, 'by every blast of false teaching, like ships without compass or rudder. False doctrines will arise as long as the world lasts, and will be many in number, varying in minor details, but in one point alone always the same — that they are strange, new, foreign and departing from the gospel of Christ. They exist now. They will always be found within the visible church. Remember this, and do not be carried away.' Such is Paul's warning.

The apostle's warning does not stand alone. Even in the midst of the Sermon on the Mount there fell from the loving lips of our Saviour a solemn caution: 'Beware of false prophets, who come to you in sheep's clothing, but inwardly they are ravenous wolves' (Matt. 7:15). Even in Paul's last address to the Ephesian elders, though he finds no time to speak about the sacraments, he does find time to warn his friends against false doctrine: 'Also from among yourselves men will rise up, speaking perverse things, to draw away the disciples after themselves' (Acts 20:30).

What does the Second Epistle to the Corinthians say? 'I fear, lest somehow, as the serpent deceived Eve by his craftiness, so your minds may be corrupted from the simplicity that is in Christ' (2 Cor. 11:3).

What does the Epistle to the Galatians say? 'I marvel that you are turning away so soon from him who called you in the grace of Christ, to a different gospel' (Gal. 1:6). 'Who has bewitched you?... Having begun in the Spirit, are you now being made perfect by the flesh?' (Gal. 3:1,3). 'How is it that you turn again to the weak and beggarly elements...? ...You observe days and months and seasons and years. I am afraid for you' (Gal. 4:9-11). 'Stand fast therefore in the liberty by which Christ has made us free, and do not be entangled again by a yoke of bondage' (Gal. 5:1).

What does the Epistle to the Ephesians say? 'We should no longer be children, tossed to and fro and carried about with every wind of doctrine' (Eph. 4:14).

What does the Epistle to the Colossians say? 'Beware lest anyone cheat you through philosophy and empty deceit, according to the tradition of men, according to the basic principles of the world, and not according to Christ' (Col. 2:8).

What does the First Epistle to Timothy say? 'The Spirit expressly says that in latter times some will depart from the faith' (1 Tim. 4:1).

What does the Second Epistle of Peter say? 'There will be false teachers among you, who will secretly bring in destructive heresies' (2 Peter 2:1).

What does the First Epistle of John say? 'Do not believe every spirit ... many false prophets have gone out into the world' (1 John 4:1).

What does the Epistle of Jude say? 'Contend earnestly for the faith which was once for all delivered to the saints. For certain men have crept in unnoticed' (Jude 1:3-4).

Let us take good note of these texts. These things were written for our learning.

What shall we say about these texts? How they may strike others, I cannot say. I only know how they strike me. To tell us, as some do, in the face of these texts, that the early churches were a model of perfection and purity is absurd. Even in apostolic days, it appears, there were numerous errors both in doctrine and practice. To tell us, as others do, that clergymen ought never to handle controversial subjects, and never to warn their people against erroneous views, is senseless and unreasonable. At this rate we might neglect much of the New Testament. Surely the dog that does not bark and the sleeping shepherd are the best allies of the wolf, the thief and the robber. It is not for nothing that Paul says, 'If you instruct the brethren in these things, you will be a good minister of Jesus Christ' (1 Tim. 4:6).

The need for such a warning

A plain warning against false doctrine is especially needed in the present day. The school of the Pharisees and the school of the Sadducees, those ancient schools of thought which had in them the seeds of every kind of harmful doctrine, were never more active than they are now. Between men adding to the truth on one side and men taking away from it on the other, between those who bury truth under additions and those who mutilate it by subtractions, between superstition and unbelief, between Roman Catholicism and liberal theology, between ritualism and rationalism — between these upper and lower millstones the gospel is very nearly crushed to death!

Strange views are continually propounded by clergymen about subjects of the deepest importance. About the atonement, the divinity of Christ, the inspiration of the Bible, the reality of miracles, the eternity of future punishment, about the church, the ministerial office, the sacraments, the confessional, the honour due to the Virgin, prayers for the dead — about all these things there is nothing too outrageous to be taught by some ministers in these days. By the pen and by the tongue, by the press and by the pulpit, we are incessantly inundated with a flood of erroneous opinions. To ignore the fact is merely to deceive ourselves. Others see it, even if we pretend to be ignorant of it. The danger is real, great and unmistakable. Never was it so necessary to say, 'Do not be carried about...'

Many things combine to make the present inroads of false doctrine especially dangerous. There is an undeniable zeal in some of the teachers of error and their 'earnestness' (to use an unfortunate expression often used to describe them) makes many think they must be right. There is a great appearance of learning and theological knowledge and many imagine that such clever and intellectual men must surely be safe guides. There is a general tendency to free thought and free enquiry in these days and many like to prove their independence of judgement by believing whatever happens to be the latest fashion. There is a widespread desire to appear charitable and liberal-minded, so that many seem half ashamed of saying that anybody can be in the wrong. There is a quantity of half-truth taught by the modern false teachers; they are constantly using scriptural terms and phrases in an unscriptural sense. There is a morbid craving in the public mind for a more ceremonial, sensational, showy form of worship with a greater appeal to the senses; men are impatient of inward, invisible work in the heart. There is a foolish readiness on all sides to believe everybody who talks cleverly, lovingly and earnestly, and a determination to forget that Satan is often transformed 'into an angel of light' (2 Cor. 11:14). There is a widespread tendency to gullibility among professing Christians; every heretic who tells his story plausibly is sure to be believed and everybody who doubts him is called a persecutor and a narrow-minded man. All these things are symptomatic of our times. I defy any observant man to deny them. They tend to make the attacks of false doctrine in our day particularly dangerous. They make it more necessary than ever to cry out, 'Do not be carried about...'

The best safeguard against false doctrine

If anyone asks me, 'What is the best safeguard against false doctrine?' I answer in one word: 'The Bible — the Bible regularly read, regularly prayed over, regularly studied.' We must go back to the old prescription of our Master: 'Search the

Scriptures' (John 5:39, AV). If we want a weapon to wield against the devious schemes of Satan, there is nothing like 'the sword of the Spirit, the Word of God'. But to wield it successfully, we must read it habitually, diligently, intelligently and prayerfully. This is a point on which, I fear, many fail. In an age of hurry and frenzied activity, few read their Bibles as much as they should. More books perhaps are read than ever, but less of the one book which makes man wise to salvation. Roman Catholicism and liberal theology could never have made such havoc in the church if there had not been a most superficial knowledge of the Scriptures throughout the land. A Bible-reading congregation is the strength of a church.

'Search the Scriptures.' Note how the Lord Jesus Christ and his apostles continually refer to the Old Testament as a document just as authoritative as the New. Note how they quote texts from the Old Testament, as the voice of God, as if every word was given by inspiration. Note how the greatest miracles in the Old Testament are all referred to in the New, as unquestioned and unquestionable facts. Note how all the leading events in the Pentateuch are constantly spoken of as historical events, the reality of which admits of no dispute. Note how the atonement and substitution and sacrifice run through the whole Bible, from first to last, as essential doctrines of revelation. Note how the resurrection of Christ, the greatest of all miracles, is proved by such an overwhelming mass of evidence that the one who refuses to believe it may as well say he will believe no evidence at all. Take good note of all these things, and you will find it very hard to be a rationalist! The difficulties surrounding unbelief are very great; a man needs to be more credulous to be an unbeliever than to be a Christian. But the difficulties of rationalism are greater still. Freedom in handling Scripture, the results of modern criticism, a broad and liberal theology — all these are fine, pompous, high-sounding phrases, which please some minds and look very impressive from a distance. But the man who looks below the surface of things will soon find that there is no sure standing-ground between extreme rationalism and atheism.

'Search the Scriptures.' Note what a conspicuous absence there is in the New Testament of what may be called the sacramental system, and the whole circle of ritualistic theology. Note how extremely little is said there about the effects of baptism. Note how very seldom the Lord's Supper is mentioned in the epistles. Find, if you can, a single text in which New Testament ministers are called sacrificing priests, or the Lord's Supper is called a sacrifice, or private confession to ministers is recommended and practised. Turn, if you can, to one single verse in which sacrificial vestments are named as desirable, or in which lighted candles and pots of flowers on the Lord's Table, or processions, incense, flags and banners, turning to the east and bowing down to the bread and wine, or prayer to the Virgin Mary and the angels, are sanctioned. Take good note of these things, and you will find it very hard to be a ritualist! You may find your authority for ritualism in garbled quotations from the Church Fathers, in long extracts from monastic, mystical, or Roman Catholic writers, but you certainly will not find it in the Bible. Between the plain Bible, honestly and fairly interpreted, and extreme ritualism there is a gulf which cannot be passed.

If we would not be 'carried about with various and strange doctrines,' we must remember the words of our Lord Jesus Christ: 'Search the Scriptures.' Ignorance of the Bible is the root of all error. Knowledge of the Bible is the best antidote against modern heresies.

2. A valuable prescription

I now proceed to examine Paul's valuable prescription: 'It is good that the heart be established by grace, not with foods.'

There are two words in this prescription which require a little explanation. A right understanding of them is absolutely essential to a proper use of the apostle's advice. One of these words is 'foods', and the other is 'grace'.

What is meant by 'foods'?

To see the full force of the word 'foods' we must remember the immense importance attached by many Jewish Christians to the distinctions of the ceremonial law about food. The flesh of some animals and birds, according to Leviticus, might be eaten, and that of others might not be eaten. Some foods were, consequently, called 'clean', and others were called 'unclean'. To eat certain kinds of flesh made a Jew ceremonially defiled before God, and no strict Jew would touch and eat such food on any account.

Now, were these distinctions still to be kept up after Christ ascended into heaven, or were they done away with by the gospel? Were Gentile converts under any obligation to attend to the ceremonial of the Levitical law about food? Were Jewish Christians obliged to be as strict about the foods they ate as they were before Christ died and the veil of the temple was torn in two? Was the ceremonial law about foods entirely done away with, or was it not? Was the conscience of a believer in the Lord Jesus to be troubled with fear in case his food should defile him?

Questions like these appear to have formed one of the great subjects of controversy in apostolic times. As is often the case, they assumed a place entirely out of proportion to their real importance. The apostle Paul found it necessary to handle the subject in no less than three of his epistles to the churches. 'Food,' he says, 'does not commend us to God' (1 Cor. 8:8). 'The kingdom of God is not food and drink' (Rom. 14:17). 'Let no one judge you in food or in drink' (Col. 2:16). Nothing shows the fallen nature of man so clearly as the readiness of over-sensitive and scrupulous consciences to turn trifles into serious things. At last the controversy seems to have spread so far and grown to such dimensions that 'foods' came to be used as an expression to denote any ceremonial thing added to the gospel as being a thing of primary importance, any ritualistic practice, however trivial, that, instead of being left in its lawful place, came to be thrust into prominence and magnified into an essential of religion. In this sense, I believe, the word must be taken in the text now before us. By 'foods' Paul means ceremonial observances, either entirely invented by man, or else built on precepts from the law of Moses which have been invalidated and superseded by the gospel. It is an expression which was well understood in the days of the apostles.

What is meant by 'grace' in this passage?

The word 'grace,' on the other hand, seems to be employed as a comprehensive description of the whole gospel of Jesus Christ. Of that glorious gospel, grace is the main feature — grace in the original scheme, grace in the execution of it and grace in the application of it to the soul of man. Grace is the fountain of life from which our salvation flows. Grace is the agency through which our spiritual life is kept up. Are we justified? It is by grace (Rom. 3:24). Are we called? It is by grace (Gal. 1:15). Have we received forgiveness? It is through the riches of grace (Eph. 1:7). Have we a good hope? It is through grace (2 Thess. 2:16). Do we believe? It is through grace (Acts 18:27). Are we elect? It is by the election of grace (Rom. 11:5). Are we saved? It is by grace (Eph. 2:5). Why should I say more? The time would fail me to describe in every detail the part that grace does in the whole work of redemption. No wonder that Paul says to the Romans, 'We are not under law but under grace' (Rom. 6:15) and tells Titus, 'The grace of God that brings salvation has appeared to all men' (Titus 2:11).

How the heart is to be established

Such are the two great principles which Paul puts in strong contrast in the prescription we are now considering. He places opposite to one another 'foods' and 'grace' — ceremonialism and the gospel, ritualism and the free love of God in Christ Jesus. And then he lays down the great principle that it is by 'grace', and 'not foods', that the heart must be established.

Now an 'established' heart is one of the things most needed by many professing Christians. It is especially sought after by those whose knowledge is imperfect and whose conscience is only half enlightened. Such persons often feel in themselves much indwelling sin and at the same time see only very indistinctly God's remedy and Christ's fulness. Their faith is feeble, their hope dim and their consolations small. They want to experience a greater sense of comfort. They imagine they ought to feel more and see more. They are not at ease. They cannot attain to joy and peace in believing. Where should they turn? What will set their consciences at rest?

Then comes the enemy of souls and suggests some road as a short cut to an established heart. He hints at the value of some addition to the simple plan of the gospel, something that man has devised, some exaggeration of a truth, some invention to satisfy the flesh, some improvement on the old path, and whispers, 'Only use this, and your heart will be established.'

Plausible offers flow in at the same time from every quarter, like quack medicines. Each has its own patrons and advocates. On every side the poor, unstable soul hears invitations to move in some particular direction and then, he is told, his heart will be perfectly established.

'Come to us,' says the Roman Catholic. 'Join the Catholic Church, the church on the rock, the one, true, holy church, the church that cannot err. Come to her open arms, and find rest for your soul in her protection. Come to us, and your heart will be established.'

'Come to us,' says the advocate of extreme ritualism. 'You need higher and fuller views of the priesthood and the sacraments, of the real presence in the Lord's Supper, of the soothing influence of daily service, daily masses, of making oral confession and receiving absolution from a priest. Come and take up sound views of the church, and your heart will be established.'

'Come to us,' says the person who is passionately opposed to any link between church and state. 'Cast off the restrictions and the bonds associated with established churches. Come out from all alliance with the state. Enjoy religious liberty. Throw away orders of service and prayer books. Adopt our watchword. Cast in your lot with us, and your heart will soon be established.'

'Come to us,' say those who reject any form of church organization or an ordained ministry. 'Shake off all the bondage of creeds and churches and systems. We will soon show you higher, deeper, more exalting, more enlightened views of truth. Join us, and your heart will soon be established.'

'Come to us,' says the liberal theologian. 'Discard those aspects of Christianity which you can no longer accept as you would old, worn-out clothes. Give your reason free scope and play. Adopt a freer mode of handling Scripture. No longer be a slave to an ancient, primitive book. Break your chains and your heart will be established.'

Every experienced Christian is well aware that such appeals are constantly made to unsettled minds in the present day. Who has not seen that, when boldly and confidently made, they produce a painful effect on some people? Who has not observed that they often mislead unstable souls and lead them into misery for years?

'What does the Scripture say?' This is the only sure guide. Listen to what Paul says. An established heart is not to be obtained by joining this party or that. It comes 'by grace, not with foods'. Other things have 'an appearance of wisdom' perhaps, and give a temporary satisfaction to 'the flesh' (Col. 2:23). But they have no healing power about them in reality, and leave the unhappy man who trusts them no better, but rather worse.

A clearer knowledge of the divine scheme of grace, its eternal purposes and its application to man by Christ's redeeming work; a firmer grasp of the doctrine of grace, of God's free love in Christ, of Christ's full and complete satisfaction for sin and of justification by simple faith; a more intimate acquaintance with Christ the giver and fountain of grace, his offices, his sympathy and his power; a more thorough experience of the inward work of grace in the heart — this, and this alone, is the grand secret of an established heart. This is the old path of peace. This is the true panacea for restless consciences. It may seem at first too simple, too easy, too cheap, too commonplace, too plain. But all the wisdom of man will never show the burdened soul a better road to rest of heart. Secret pride and self-righteousness, I fear, are too often the reason why this good old road is not used.

I believe there never was a time when it was more necessary to advocate the old apostolic prescription than it is in the present day. Never were there so many unestablished and unsettled Christians wandering about, and tossed to and fro, from lack of knowledge. Never was it so important for faithful ministers to set the trumpet to their mouths and proclaim everywhere, 'Grace, grace, grace, not foods, establishes the heart.'

From the days of the apostles there has never been any shortage of spiritual quack doctors, who have professed to heal the wounds of conscience with man-made remedies.

In the Anglican Church there have always been some who have in their hearts turned back to Egypt and, not content with the simplicity of the worship, have hankered after the ceremonial delicacies of the church of Rome. Archbishop Laud, of unhappy memory, did a little in this way, but what he did was nothing compared with what some clergymen in more recent times have done. To hear the sacraments incessantly exalted, and preaching disparaged, to see the Lord's Supper turned into an object of idolatrous worship under the pretext of making it more honourable, to find the plain form of worship prescribed in the Prayer Book overlaid with so many new-fangled ornaments and ceremonies that its essentials are quite buried — how common all this is! These things were once a pestilence that walked in darkness. They are now a destruction that lays waste at noonday. They are the joy of our enemies, the sorrow of the church's most faithful members, the damage of Christianity in England, the plague of our times. And to what may they all be traced? To neglect or forgetfulness of Paul's simple prescription: it is grace, and not foods, that establishes the heart.

Let us take care that *in our own personal religion*, grace is all. Let us have clear systematic views of the gospel of the grace of God. Nothing else will do good in the hour of sickness, in the day of trial, on our death-beds and when we are called to pass through the overflowing river. Christ living in our hearts by faith, Christ's free grace the only foundation under the soles of our feet — this alone will give peace. Once let in self and formal rituals and man's inventions as a necessary part of our religion, and we are on a quicksand. We may be amused, excited, or kept quiet for a time, like children with toys, by a religion of 'foods'. Such a religion has 'an appearance of wisdom'. But unless our religion is one in which 'grace' is everything, we shall never feel that we are established.

3. An instructive fact

In the last place, I proceed to examine the instructive fact which Paul records. He says, 'Foods ... have not profited those who have been occupied with them.'

We have no means of knowing whether the apostle, in using this language, referred to any particular churches or individuals. Of course it is possible that he had in view the Christians of Antioch and Galatia who were advocating a return to the practices of Judaism, or the Ephesians of whom he speaks to Timothy in his Pastoral Epistle, or the Colossians who caused him so much inward conflict, or the Hebrew believers who were to be found in every church without exception.

It seems to me far more probable, however, that he had no particular church or churches in view. I rather think that he makes a broad, general, sweeping statement about all who in any place had exalted ceremonial at the expense of the doctrines of 'grace'. And he makes a general declaration about them all. They have got no good from their favourite notions. They have not been more inwardly happy, more outwardly holy, or more generally useful. Their religion has been most unprofitable to them. Man-made alterations of God's precious medicine for sinners, man-made additions to Christ's glorious gospel, however cleverly defended and plausibly supported, do no real good to those who adopt them. They confer no increased inward comfort; they bring no growth of real holiness; they give no increased usefulness to the church and the world. Calmly, quietly and mildly, but firmly, decidedly and unflinchingly, the assertion is made, 'Foods have *not profited* those who have been occupied with them.'

The evidence of church history

The whole stream of church history abundantly confirms the truth of the apostle's position. Who has not heard of the hermits and ascetics of the early centuries? Who has not heard of the monks and nuns and recluses of the Roman church in the middle ages? Who has not heard of the burning zeal, the devoted self-denial of Roman Catholics like Xavier and Ignatius

Loyola? The earnestness, the fervour, the self-sacrifice of all these people are matters beyond dispute. But none who reads carefully and intelligently the records of their lives — even some of the best of them — can fail to see that they had no solid peace or inward rest of soul. Their very feverish restlessness is enough to show that their consciences were not at ease. No one can fail to see that, with all their passionate zeal and self-denial, they never did much good to the world. They gathered round themselves admiring supporters. They left behind a high reputation for self-denial and sincerity. They made men wonder at them while they lived and sometimes canonize them when they died. But they did nothing to *convert souls*. And what is the reason for this? They attached an excessive importance to man-made ritual and ceremonial, and made less than they ought to have done of the gospel of the grace of God. Their principle was to make much of 'foods' and little of 'grace'. Hence they verified the words of Paul: 'Foods have *not profited* those who have been occupied with them.'

In more recent times we have seen a striking testimony to the truth of Paul's assertion when large numbers of clergymen seceded from the Church of England and joined the church of Rome. They wanted more of what they called Catholic doctrine and Catholic ceremonial. They honestly acted up to their principles, and went over to Rome. They were not all weak, illiterate, second-rate and inferior men; several of them were men of impressive talents, whose gifts would have won for them a high position in any profession. Yet what did they gain by the step they took? What profit did they find in leaving 'grace' for 'foods', in exchanging Protestantism for Catholicism? Did they attain a higher standard of holiness? Did they procure for themselves a greater degree of usefulness?

Let one of these men supply an answer. Mr Ffoulkes, one of those who led the way, later openly declared that the preaching of some of his fellow 'converts' to Catholicism was not so powerful as it was when they were English churchmen and that the highest degree of holy living he had ever seen was not to be found within the Roman Catholic Church, but in the quiet parsonages and unpretending family life of godly English clergymen! Intentionally or unintentionally, wittingly or unwittingly, meaning it or not meaning it, nothing can be more striking than the testimony Mr Ffoulkes bears to the truth of the apostle's assertion: foods do not profit even those who make a great fuss about them. The religious system which exalts ceremonial observances and man-made ritual does no real good to its adherents, compared to the simple old gospel of the grace of God.

Let us turn now, for a few moments, to the other side of the picture, and see what 'grace' has done. Let us hear how profitable the doctrines of the gospel have proved to those who have clung firmly to them and have not tried to mend and improve and patch them up by adding, as essentials, the 'foods' of man-made rituals.

It was 'grace, not ... foods' that made Martin Luther do the work that he did in the world. The key to all his success was his constant declaration of justification by faith, without the deeds of the law. This was the truth which enabled him to break the chains of Rome and let light into Europe.

It was 'grace, not ... foods' that made the English martyrs Latimer and Hooper exercise so mighty an influence in life and shine so brightly in death. They saw clearly, and taught plainly, the true priesthood of Christ and salvation only by grace. They honoured God's grace and God put honour on them.

It was 'grace, not ... foods' that made Romaine and Venn and their companions turn the world upside down in England in the eighteenth century. In themselves they were not men of extraordinary learning or intellectual power. But they revived and brought out again the real, pure doctrines of grace.

It was 'grace, not … foods' that made Simeon and Daniel
Wilson and Bickersteth such striking instruments of usefulness in the first half of the nineteenth century. God's free grace
was the great truth on which they relied and which they continually brought forward. For so doing God put honour on
them. They made much of God's grace and the God of grace
made much of them.

The list of biographies of ministers tells a striking tale. Who
are those who have shaken the world and left their mark on
their generation and aroused consciences and converted sinners and edified saints? Not those who have made asceticism
and rituals and sacraments and services and ordinances the
main thing; but those who have made the most of God's free
grace! In a day of strife, controversy, doubt and perplexity,
men forget this. Facts are stubborn things. Let us look calmly
at them and not be moved by those who tell us that daily services, processions, incense, ritual bowing, making the sign of
the cross, going to confession, receiving absolution, and the
like, are the secret of a prosperous Christianity. Let us look at
plain facts. Facts in old history and facts in more recent days,
facts wherever we look about us, support the assertion of Paul.
The religion of 'foods' does not profit those who are occupied with them. It is the religion of 'grace' that brings inward
peace, outward holiness and general usefulness.

A few words of practical application

Let me wind up this chapter with a few words of practical
application. We are living in a particularly dangerous age in
matters of religion. I am quite sure that the advice I am going
to offer deserves serious attention.

In the first place, *let us not be surprised at the rise and
progress of false doctrine.* It is an old thing, so old that it goes

back to the time of the apostles. It began before they died. They predicted that there would be plenty of it before the end of the world. It is wisely ordered by God for the testing of our grace and to prove who has real faith. If there were no such thing as false doctrine or heresy on earth, I should begin to think the Bible was not true.

Secondly, *let us make up our minds to resist false doctrine* and not to be carried away by fashion and bad example. Let us not flinch because all around us, high and low, rich and poor, are swept away, like geese in a flood, before a torrent of false teaching. Let us be firm and stand our ground.

Let us resist false doctrine and contend earnestly for the faith once for all delivered to the saints. Let us not be ashamed of showing our colours and standing out for New Testament truth. Let us not be stopped by the foolish cry of 'controversy'. The thief likes dogs that do not bark and watchmen that give no alarm. The devil is a thief and a robber. If we hold our peace, and do not resist false doctrine, we please him and displease God.

Thirdly, *let us try to preserve the old Protestant principles of the Church of England* and to hand them down undamaged to our grandchildren. The Church of England is worth fighting for. She has done good service in days gone by and she may yet do more, if we can keep her free from Roman Catholicism and unbelief. Once readmit and sanction the Roman Catholic mass and confession to priests, and the Church of England will be ruined. Then let us fight hard for the Church of England being kept a Protestant church. Let us read the Thirty-Nine Articles with attention and learn from these articles what are the real principles of the church. Let us arm our memories with these articles and be able to quote them. Before the cutting edge and sharpened point of these articles, fairly interpreted, the advocates of extreme ritualism and rationalism can never stand their ground.

Fourthly and lastly, *let us make sure work of our own per-sonal salvation.* Let us seek to know and feel that we our-selves are 'saved'. The day of controversy is always a day of spiritual danger. Men are apt to confound orthodoxy with con-version, and to imagine that they must go to heaven if they know how to answer those who teach false doctrine. Yet neither mere earnestness without knowledge nor mere head-knowl-edge of evangelical truth saves anyone. Let us never forget this. Let us not rest till we feel the blood of Christ sprinkled on our consciences and have the witness of the Spirit within us that we are born again. This is reality. This is true religion. This will last. This will never fail us. It is the possession of grace in the heart, and not the intellectual knowledge of it, that profits and saves the soul.

6.
The fallibility of ministers

'But when Peter had come to Antioch, I withstood him to his face, because he was to be blamed; for before certain men came from James, he would eat with the Gentiles; but when they came, he withdrew and separated himself, fearing those who were of the circumcision. And the rest of the Jews also played the hypocrite with him, so that even Barnabas was carried away with their hypocrisy. But when I saw that they were not straightforward about the truth of the gospel, I said to Peter before them all, "If you, being a Jew, live in the manner of Gentiles and not as the Jews, why do you compel Gentiles to live as Jews? We who are Jews by nature, and not sinners of the Gentiles, knowing that a man is not justified by the works of the law but by faith in Jesus Christ, even we have believed in Christ Jesus, that we might be justified by faith in Christ and not by the works of the law; for by the works of the law no flesh shall be justified"' (Gal. 2:11-16).

Have we ever considered what the apostle Peter did at Antioch? It is a question that deserves serious consideration.

We are often told what the apostle Peter did at *Rome*, although we have hardly a scrap of authentic information about it. Legends, traditions and fables abound on the subject. But, unhappily for these writers, Scripture is utterly silent upon the point. There is nothing in Scripture to show that the apostle Peter ever was at Rome at all!

But what did the apostle Peter do at *Antioch*? This is the point to which I want to direct attention. This is the subject of the passage from the Epistle to the Galatians which is quoted at the head of this chapter. On this point, at any rate, the Scripture speaks clearly and unmistakably.

The six verses of the passage before us are striking on many accounts. They are striking if we consider the *event* which they describe: here is one apostle rebuking another! They are striking when we consider *who the two men are*: Paul, the younger, rebukes Peter, the elder! They are striking, when we remark *the occasion*: this was no glaring fault, no flagrant sin, at first sight, that Peter had committed! Yet the apostle Paul says, 'I withstood him to his face, because he was to be blamed.' He does more than this: he reproves Peter publicly for his error in front of all the church at Antioch. He goes even further: he writes an account of the matter which is now read in hundreds of different languages all over the world.

It is my firm conviction that the Holy Spirit means us to take particular notice of this passage of Scripture. If Christianity had been an invention of man, these things would never have been recorded. An impostor would have hushed up the difference between two apostles. The Spirit of truth has caused these verses to be written for our learning, and we shall do well to pay careful attention to their contents.

There are three great lessons from Antioch which I think we ought to learn from this passage.

1. The first lesson is that great ministers may make great mistakes.
2. The second is that to keep the truth of Christ in his church is even more important than to keep peace.
3. The third is that there is no doctrine which we ought to guard so jealously as justification by faith without the deeds of the law.

1. Great ministers may make great mistakes

The first great lesson we learn from Antioch is that great ministers may make great mistakes. What clearer proof of it can we have than that which is set before us in this passage?

Peter, without doubt, was one of the greatest in the company of the apostles. He was an old disciple. He was a disciple who had had special advantages and privileges. He had been a constant companion of the Lord Jesus. He had heard the Lord preach, seen the Lord work miracles, enjoyed the benefit of the Lord's private teaching, been numbered among the Lord's intimate friends and gone out and come in with him all the time he ministered on earth. He was the apostle to whom the keys of the kingdom of heaven were given, and by whose hand those keys were first used. He was the first who opened the door of faith to the Jews, by preaching to them on the Day of Pentecost. He was the first who opened the door of faith to the Gentiles, by going to the house of Cornelius and receiving him into the church. He was the first to rise up in the council in Acts chapter 15 and say, 'Why do you test God by putting a yoke on the neck of the disciples which neither our fathers nor we were able to bear?'

And yet here this very Peter, this same apostle, plainly falls into a great mistake. The apostle Paul tells us, 'I withstood him to his face.' He tells us that 'He was to be blamed.' He says he feared 'those who were of the circumcision'. He says of him and his companions that 'They were not were not straightforward about the truth of the gospel.' He speaks of their 'hypocrisy'. He tells us that even Barnabas, his old companion in missionary labours, 'was carried away' by this hypocrisy. What a striking fact this is — this is Simon Peter! This is the third great error of his which the Holy Spirit has thought fit to record! Once we find him trying to keep back our Lord, as far as he could, from the great work of the cross

and being severely rebuked. Then we find him denying the
Lord three times and with an oath. Here again we find him
endangering the leading truth of Christ's gospel. Surely we
may say, 'Lord, what is man?' The church of Rome boasts
that the apostle Peter is her founder and first bishop. Very
well, let us grant for the moment that it is so; let us only remember that of all the apostles there is not one, except, of
course, Judas Iscariot, of whom we have so many proofs that
he was a fallible man.[1]

But it is all meant to teach us that even the apostles themselves, when not writing under the inspiration of the Holy Spirit,
were at times liable to make mistakes. It is meant to teach us
that the best men are weak and fallible so long as they are in
the body. Unless the grace of God holds them up, any one of
them may go astray at any time. It is very humbling, but it is
very true. True Christians are converted, justified and sanctified. They are living members of Christ, beloved children of
God and heirs of eternal life. They are elect, chosen, called
and kept unto salvation. They have the Spirit. But they are *not*
infallible.

Will not *rank and dignity* confer infallibility? No, they will
not! It does not matter in the slightest what a man is called. He
may be a tsar, an emperor, a king, a prince. He may be a pope
or a cardinal, an archbishop or a bishop, a dean or an archdeacon, a minister or a deacon. He is still a fallible man. Neither
the crown, nor the tiara, nor the anointing oil, nor the mitre,
nor the laying on of hands can prevent a man from making
mistakes.

---

1. It is curious to observe the measures to which some writers have been re-
duced, in order to explain away the plain meaning of the verses quoted at the
head of this chapter. Some have maintained that Paul did not really rebuke Peter,
but only pretended to do so, for show and to keep up appearances! Others have
maintained that it was not Peter the apostle who was rebuked, but another Peter,
one of the seventy! Such interpretations need no comment. They are simply absurd. The truth is that the plain, honest meaning of the verses strikes a heavy
blow at the favourite Roman Catholic doctrine of the primacy and superiority of
Peter over the rest of the apostles.

Will not *numbers* confer infallibility? No, they will not! You may gather together princes by the score and ministers by the hundred, but when gathered together, they are still liable to make mistakes. You may call them a council, or a synod, or an assembly, or a conference, or what you like. It does not matter in the least. Their conclusions are still the conclusions of fallible men. Their collective wisdom is still capable of making enormous mistakes. The Twenty-First Article of the Church of England is right when it says, 'General councils may err, and sometimes have erred, even in things [relating to] God.'

The example of the apostle Peter at Antioch is one that does not stand alone. It is only a parallel of many cases that we find written for our learning in Holy Scripture. Do we not remember Abraham, the father of the faithful, following the advice of Sarah and taking Hagar for a wife? Do we not remember Aaron, the first high priest, listening to the Israelites and making a golden calf? Do we not remember Nathan the prophet telling David to build a temple? Do we not remember Solomon, the wisest of men, allowing his wives to build their high places of false worship? Do we not remember Asa, the good King of Judah, seeking, not the Lord, but the physicians? Do we not remember Jehoshaphat, the good king, going down to help the wicked Ahab? Do we not remember Hezekiah, the good king, receiving the ambassadors of Babylon? Do we not remember Josiah, the last of Judah's good kings, going out to fight with Pharaoh? Do we not remember James and John wanting fire to come down from heaven? These things deserve to be remembered. They were not written without cause. They loudly proclaim, 'No man is infallible!'

And who does not see, when he reads the history of the church of Christ, repeated proofs that the best of men can make mistakes? The early Church Fathers were zealous according to their knowledge and ready to die for Christ. But many of them were in favour of monasticism, and nearly all sowed the seeds of many superstitions.

The Reformers were honoured instruments in the hand of God for reviving the cause of truth on earth. Yet hardly one of them can be named who did not make some great mistake. Martin Luther held tenaciously to the doctrine of consubstantiation [i.e. that during the communion service the actual body and blood of Christ were in some way physically present in the bread and wine]. Melanchthon was often timid and undecided. Calvin allowed Servetus to be burned. Cranmer recanted and fell away for a time from his first faith. Jewell subscribed to Roman Catholic doctrines for fear of death. Hooper disturbed the Church of England by making too great an issue over the question of vestments. The Puritans, in later times, denounced freedom of worship as the work of the devil. Wesley and Toplady, in the eighteenth century, abused each other in most shameful language. Irving, in the nineteenth century, gave way to the delusion of speaking in unknown tongues. All these things speak with a loud voice. They all lift up a beacon to the church of Christ. They all say, 'Stop trusting in man' (Isa. 2:22, NIV) 'Call no man your master.' 'Do not call anyone on earth your father' (Matt. 23:9). 'Let no one glory in men' (1 Cor. 3:21). 'He who glories, let him glory in the Lord' (2 Cor. 10:17). They all cry, 'No man is infallible!'

The lesson is one that we all need. We are all naturally inclined to lean upon man, whom we can see, rather than upon God, whom we cannot see. We naturally love to lean upon the ministers of the visible church, rather than upon the Lord Jesus Christ, the great Shepherd and Overseer and High Priest, who is invisible. We need to be continually warned and put on our guard.

I see this tendency to lean on man everywhere. I know no branch of the Protestant church of Christ which does not require to be cautioned upon the point. It is a snare, for example, for those of us in the Anglican tradition to make idols of Bishop Pearson and the wise Bishop Hooker. It is a snare for the

Scottish Presbyterian to pin his faith on John Knox, the Covenanters and Dr Chalmers. It is a snare to the Methodists to worship the memory of John Wesley. It is a snare to the Congregationalist to see no fault in any opinion of Owen and Doddridge. It is a snare to the Baptist to exaggerate the wisdom of Gill and Fuller and Robert Hall. All these are snares, and into these snares how many fall!

We all naturally love to have a pope of our own. We are far too ready to think that because some great minister or some learned man says a thing — or because our own minister, whom we love, says a thing — it must be right, without examining whether it is in Scripture or not. Most men dislike the trouble of thinking for themselves. They like following a leader. They are like sheep: when one goes over the hill all the rest follow. Here at Antioch even Barnabas was carried away. We can well imagine that good man saying, 'An old apostle, like Peter, surely cannot be wrong. Following him, I cannot go wrong.'

And now let us see what practical lessons we may learn from this part of our subject.

The early church was not infallible

For one thing, let us learn not to put implicit confidence in any man's opinion, merely because he lived many hundreds of years ago. Peter was a man who lived in the time of Christ himself, and yet he could make mistakes.

There are many who often talk about what the early church said and did. They would have us believe that those who lived nearest to the time of the apostles must of course know more about truth than we can. There is no foundation for any such opinion. It is a fact that the most ancient writers in the church of Christ are often at variance with one another. It is a fact that they often changed their own minds and retracted their own former opinions. It is a fact that they often wrote foolish and weak things and often showed great ignorance in their explanations of Scripture. It is pointless to expect to find them to be free from mistakes. Infallibility is not to be found in the early fathers, but in the Bible.

Ministers are not infallible

For another thing, let us learn not to put implicit confidence in any man's opinion, merely because of his office as a minister. Peter was one of the very chief of the apostles, and yet he could make mistakes.

This is a point on which men have continually gone astray. It is the rock on which the early church struck. Men soon took up the saying: 'Do nothing contrary to the opinion of the bishop.' But what are bishops, or priests, or deacons? What are the best of ministers but men — dust, ashes and clay — men with a nature like our own, men exposed to temptations, men liable to weaknesses and failings? What does the Scripture say? 'Who then is Paul, and who is Apollos, but ministers through whom you believed, as the Lord gave to each one?' (1 Cor. 3:5).

Bishops have often driven the truth into the wilderness, and decreed that to be true which was false. The greatest errors have been begun by ministers. Hophni and Phinehas, the sons of the high priest, made religion something to be detested by the Israelites. Annas and Caiaphas, though in the direct line of descent from Aaron, crucified the Lord. Arius, that great arch-heretic who denied the divinity of Christ, was a minister. It is absurd to suppose that ordained men cannot go wrong. We should follow them so far as they teach according to the Bible, but no further. We should believe them so long as they can say, 'This is what is written...', 'Thus says the Lord...,' but further than this we are not to go. Infallibility is not to be found in ordained men, but in the Bible.

Learned men are not infallible

For another thing, let us learn not to place implicit confidence in any man's opinion, merely because of his learning. Peter was a man who had miraculous gifts, and could speak with tongues, and yet he could make mistakes.

This again is a point on which many go wrong. This is the rock on which men struck in the Middle Ages. Men looked on Thomas Aquinas and Duns Scotus and Peter Lombard, and many of their companions, as almost inspired. They gave some of them flattering epithets in token of their admiration. They talked of 'the unanswerable Dr ...' 'the angelic' teacher, 'the incomparable' professor, and seemed to think that whatever these learned men said must be true! But what is the most learned of men, if he is not taught by the Holy Spirit? What is the most learned of all theologians but a mere fallible descendant of Adam at his very best? Vast knowledge of books and great ignorance of God's truth may go side by side. They have done so, they may do so and they will do so in all times. I will go so far as to say that the two volumes of Robert Murray M'Cheyne's *Memoirs and Sermons* have done more positive good to the souls of men than any large folio work that Origen or Cyprian ever wrote. I do not doubt that the one volume of *Pilgrim's Progress,* written by a man who knew hardly any book but his Bible and was ignorant of Greek and Latin, will prove in the last day to have done more for the benefit of the world than all the works of the medieval theologians put together.

Learning is a gift that ought not to be despised. It is an evil day when books are not valued in the church. But it is amazing to observe how vast a man's intellectual attainments may be, and yet how little he may know of the grace of God. I have no doubt the authorities of Oxford University in the eighteenth century knew more of Hebrew, Greek and Latin than

John Wesley, George Whitefield, John Berridge or Henry Venn.
But they knew little of the gospel of Christ. Infallibility is not
to be found among learned men, but in the Bible.

Even godly ministers are not infallible

For another thing, let us take care that we do not place implicit confidence on our own minister's opinion, however godly
he may be. Peter was a man of mighty grace, and yet he could
make mistakes.

Your minister may indeed be a man of God, and worthy of
all honour for his preaching and example, but do not make a
pope of him. Do not place his word side by side with the Word
of God. Do not spoil him by flattery. Do not let him suppose
he can make no mistakes. Do not lean your whole weight on
his opinion, or you may find to your cost that he can make
mistakes.

It is written of Joash, King of Judah, that he 'did what was
right in the sight of the Lord all the years of Jehoiada the priest'
(2 Chron. 24:2). Jehoiada died and then the religion of Joash
died too. In just the same way, your minister may die and then
your religion may die too. He may change and your religion
may change. He may go away and your religion may go. Oh,
do not be satisfied with a religion built on a man! Do not be
content with saying, 'I have hope, because my own minister
has told me that...' Seek to be able to say, 'I have hope, because I find it written in the Word of God that...' If your peace
is to be solid, you must go to the fountain of all truth yourself.
If your comforts are to be lasting, you must visit the well of
life yourself and draw fresh water for your own soul. Ministers may depart from the faith. The visible church may be broken up. But the one who has the Word of God written in his
heart has a foundation beneath his feet which will never fail
him. Honour your minister as a faithful ambassador of Christ.

Esteem him very highly in love for his work's sake. But never forget that infallibility is not to be found in godly ministers, but in the Bible.

The things I have mentioned are worth remembering. Let us bear them in mind, and we shall have learned one lesson from Antioch.

2. To keep the truth of Christ in his church is even more important than to keep peace

I now pass on to the second lesson that we learn from Antioch. That lesson is that to keep gospel truth in the church is of even greater importance than to keep peace.

I suppose no one knew better the value of peace and unity than the apostle Paul. He was the apostle who wrote to the Corinthians about love. He was the apostle who said, 'Be of the same mind towards one another' (Rom. 12:16). 'Be at peace among yourselves' (1 Thess. 5:13). 'Let us be of the same mind' (Phil. 3:16). 'A servant of the Lord must not quarrel' (2 Tim. 2:24). 'There is one body and one Spirit, just as you were called in one hope of your calling; one Lord, one faith, one baptism' (Eph. 4:4-5). He was the apostle who said, 'I have become all things to all men, that I might by all means save some' (1 Cor. 9:22). Yet see how he acts here! He opposes Peter to his face. He publicly rebukes him. He runs the risk of all the consequences that might follow. He takes the chance of everything that might be said by the enemies of the church at Antioch. Above all, he writes it down and records it for all time, that it never might be forgotten, that wherever the gospel is preached throughout the world, this public rebuke of an erring apostle might be known and read by all men.

Now, why did he do this? Because he dreaded false doctrine, because he knew that a little leaven leavens the whole lump, because he would teach us that we ought to contend jealously for the truth and to fear the loss of truth more than the loss of peace.

Paul's example is one we shall do well to remember in the present day. Many people will put up with anything in religion, if they may only have a quiet life. They have a morbid dread of what they call 'controversy'. They are filled with a morbid fear of what they refer to in a vague way as a 'party spirit', though they never define clearly what a 'party spirit' is. They are possessed with a morbid desire to keep the peace, and make all things smooth and pleasant, even though it may be at the expense of truth. So long as they have outward calm, smoothness, stillness and order, they seem content to give up everything else. I believe they would have thought with Ahab that Elijah was one who brought trouble on Israel, and would have helped the princes of Judah when they put Jeremiah in prison in order to stop his mouth. I have no doubt that many of these men of whom I speak would have thought that Paul at Antioch was a very imprudent man, and that he went too far!

I believe this is all wrong. We have no right to expect anything but the pure gospel of Christ, unmixed and unadulterated — the same gospel that was taught by the apostles — to do good to the souls of men. I believe that to maintain this pure truth in the church men should be ready to make any sacrifice, to hazard peace, to risk dissension and run the chance of division. They should no more tolerate false doctrine than they would tolerate sin. They should firmly resist any adding to, or taking away from, the simple message of the gospel of Christ.

For the truth's sake, our Lord Jesus Christ denounced the Pharisees, though they sat in Moses' seat and were the appointed and authorized teachers of men. 'Woe to you, scribes and Pharisees, hypocrites!' he says, eight times over, in the twenty-third chapter of Matthew. And who shall dare to breathe a suspicion that our Lord was wrong?

For the truth's sake, Paul opposed and blamed Peter, though he was a brother. Where was the use of unity when pure doctrine was gone? And who shall dare to say he was wrong?

For the truth's sake, Athanasius stood out against the world to maintain the pure doctrine about the divinity of Christ and waged a controversy with the great majority of the professing church. And who shall dare to say he was wrong?

For the truth's sake, Luther broke the unity of the church in which he was born, denounced the pope and all his ways and laid the foundation of a new teaching. And who shall dare to say that Luther was wrong?

For the truth's sake, Cranmer, Ridley and Latimer, the English Reformers, counselled Henry VIII and Edward VI to separate from Rome, and to risk the consequences of division. And who shall dare to say that they were wrong?

For the truth's sake, Whitefield and Wesley, in the eighteenth century, denounced the mere barren moral preaching of the clergy of their day, and went out into the highways and byways to save souls, well knowing that they would be cast out from the communion of their church. And who shall dare to say that they were wrong?

Yes, peace without truth is a false peace; it is the very peace of the devil. Unity without the gospel is a worthless unity; it is the very unity of hell. Let us never be ensnared by those who speak kindly of it. Let us remember the words of our Lord Jesus Christ: 'Do not think that I came to bring peace on earth. I did not come to bring peace but a sword' (Matt. 10:34). Let us remember the praise he gives to one of the churches in Revelation: 'You cannot bear those who are evil. And you have tested those who say they are apostles and are not, and

have found them liars' (Rev. 2:2). Let us remember the blame
he casts on another: 'You allow that woman Jezebel ... to
teach' (Rev. 2:20). Never let us be guilty of sacrificing any
portion of truth on the altar of peace. Let us rather be like the
Jews, who, if they found any manuscript copy of the Old
Testament Scriptures incorrect in a single letter, burned the
whole copy, rather than run the risk of losing even one tiny
fragment of the Word of God. Let us be content with nothing
short of the whole gospel of Christ.

In what way are we to make practical use of the general
principles which I have just laid down? I will give my readers
one simple piece of advice. I believe it is advice which deserves serious consideration.

I warn, then, everyone who loves his soul to be very careful as to the preaching he regularly hears, and the place of
worship he regularly attends. Anyone who deliberately settles
down under any ministry which is positively unsound is a very
unwise man. I will never hesitate to speak my mind on this
point. I am well aware that many think it a shocking thing for
a man to forsake his local parish church.[2] I cannot see with the
eyes of such people. I draw a wide distinction between teaching which is *defective* and teaching which is thoroughly *false*;
between teaching which errs on the negative side and teaching
which is positively unscriptural. But I do believe, if false doctrine is unmistakably preached in a local church, a Christian
who loves his soul is quite right in not going to that church. To
hear unscriptural teaching fifty-two Sundays in every year is a
serious thing. It is a continual dropping of slow poison into
the mind. I think it almost impossible for a man wilfully to

---

2. Here and in subsequent paragraphs Ryle particularly has in mind the system
of local parishes into which the Church of England is divided, under which every
community comes under the jurisdiction of a particular local church, with its
own clergy. However, the principles he lays down would apply to any local church
of any denomination and the local population living in the immediate vicinity of
that church.

submit himself to it, and not suffer harm. I see in the New Testament that we are plainly told to 'test all things' and 'hold fast what is good' (1 Thess. 5:21). I see in the book of Proverbs that we are commanded to 'Cease ... to hear the instruction that causeth to err from the words of knowledge' (Prov. 19:27, AV). If these words do not justify a man in ceasing to worship at a church, if positively false doctrine is preached in it, I do not know what words can.

Does anyone mean to tell us that to attend the local church is absolutely necessary to a man's salvation? If there is anyone who says so, let him come forward publicly, and give us his name. Does anyone mean to tell us that going to the local church will save any man's soul, if he dies unconverted and ignorant of Christ? If there is anyone who says so, let him come forward publicly, and give us his name. Does anyone mean to tell us that going to the local parish church will teach a man anything about Christ, or conversion, or faith, or repentance, if these subjects are hardly ever named in his local church and never properly explained? If there is anyone who says so, let him come forward publicly, and give us his name. Does anyone mean to say that a man who repents, believes in Christ, is converted and holy, will lose his soul, because he has forsaken his local parish church and learned his religion elsewhere? If there is anyone who says so, let him come forward publicly, and give us his name. For my part I detest such monstrous and extravagant ideas. I do not see the slightest foundation for them in the Word of God. I trust that the number of those who deliberately hold them is extremely small.

There are a number of parish churches where the religious teaching is little better than Roman Catholicism. Ought the local people who live in those parishes to sit still under such ministry, be content and take it quietly? They ought not. Why not? Because, like Paul, they ought to prefer truth to peace. There are a number of parish churches where the religious teaching is little better than morality. The distinctive doctrines of Christianity are never clearly proclaimed. Plato, or Seneca, or Confucius, could have taught almost as much. Ought the local people who live in those parishes to sit still under such a ministry, be content, and take it quietly? They ought not. Why not? Because, like Paul, they ought to prefer truth to peace.

I know I am using strong language in dealing with this part of my subject. I know I am treading on delicate ground. I know I am handling matters which are generally let alone, and passed over in silence. I say what I do from a sense of duty to the church of which I am a minister. I believe the state of the times and the position of the ordinary people in some parts of the country require plain speaking. Souls are perishing, in many areas, in ignorance. Honest members of the Church of England, in many districts, are disgusted and perplexed. This is no time for smooth words. I am not ignorant of those words which are constantly invoked: 'the parochial system [i.e. the system of local parishes], order, division, schism, unity, controversy', and so on. I know the cramping, silencing influence which they seem to exercise on some minds. I too have considered those expressions calmly and deliberately, and on each of them I am prepared to speak my mind.

Firstly, the parochial system is an admirable thing in theory. Let it only be well administered, and worked by truly spiritual ministers, and it is calculated to confer the greatest blessings on the nation. But it is useless to expect attachment to the local parish church, when the local minister is ignorant of the gospel or a lover of the world. In such a case we must never be surprised if men forsake their local parish church, and seek truth wherever truth is to be found. If the local minister does not preach the gospel and live the gospel, the conditions on which he claims the attention of the people who live in his parish are virtually violated, and his claim to be heard is at an end. It is absurd to expect the head of a family to endanger the

souls of his children, as well as his own, for the sake of loyalty
to the local parish church. There is no mention of parishes in
the Bible, and we have no right to require men to live and die
in ignorance, in order that they may be able to say at last, 'I
always attended my local parish church.'

Secondly, divisions and separations are most objectionable
in religion. They weaken the cause of true Christianity. They
give occasion to the enemies of all godliness to blaspheme.
But before we blame people for them, we must be careful that
we lay the blame where it is deserved. False doctrine and heresy are even worse than division between churches. If people
separate themselves from teaching which is positively false
and unscriptural, they ought to be praised rather than reproved.
In such cases separation is a virtue and not a sin. It is easy to
make sneering remarks about 'itching ears', and 'love of excitement', but it is not so easy to convince a plain reader of the
Bible that it is his duty to hear false doctrine every Sunday,
when by a little exertion he can hear truth. There is a wise old
saying that the person who is really guilty of schism is the one
who caused the schism in the first place.

Thirdly, unity, quiet and order among professing Christians
are mighty blessings. They give strength, beauty and efficiency
to the cause of Christ. But even gold may be bought at too
high a price. Unity which is obtained by the sacrifice of truth is
worth nothing. It is not the unity which pleases God. The
Roman Catholic Church boasts loudly of a unity which does
not deserve the name. It is unity which is obtained by taking
away the Bible from the people, by restraining private judgement, by encouraging ignorance, by forbidding men to think
for themselves. Like the warriors of old who laid waste whole
communities, the church of Rome 'makes a solitude and calls
it peace'. There is quiet and stillness enough in the grave, but
it is not the quiet of health, but of death. It was the false prophets
who cried, 'Peace,' when there was no peace.

Fourthly, controversy in religion is a hateful thing, It is hard enough to fight the devil, the world and the flesh without private differences in our own camp. But there is one thing which is even worse than controversy, and that is false doctrine tolerated, allowed and permitted without protest or molestation. It was controversy that won the battle of Protestant Reformation. If the views that some men hold were correct, it is plain we never ought to have had any Reformation at all! For the sake of peace, we ought to have gone on worshipping the Virgin, and bowing down to images and relics to this very day! Away with such trifling! There are times when controversy is not only a duty but a benefit. Give me the mighty thunderstorm rather than the deadly malaria. The one walks in darkness and poisons us in silence and we are never safe. The other frightens and alarms for a little while. But it is soon over, and it clears the air. It is a plain scriptural duty to 'contend earnestly for the faith which was once for all delivered to the saints' (Jude 3).

I am quite aware that the things I have said are exceedingly distasteful to many minds. I believe many are content with teaching which is not the whole truth and imagine it will be 'all the same' in the end. I am sorry for them. I am convinced that nothing but *the whole truth* is likely, as a general rule, to do good to souls. I am satisfied that those who wilfully put up with anything short of the whole truth will find at last that their souls have received much damage. There are three things which men never ought to trifle with: a little poison, a little false doctrine and a little sin.

I am quite aware that when a man expresses such opinions as those I have just brought forward, there are many ready to say, 'He is no supporter of the church.' I hear such accusations unmoved. The Day of Judgement will show who were the true friends of the Church of England and who were not. I have learned over the years that if a clergyman leads a quiet life, leaves alone the unconverted part of the world and preaches so as to offend none and edify none, he will be called by many a good minister. And I have also learned that if a man studies the Thirty-Nine Articles, labours continually for the conversion of souls, adheres closely to the great principles of the Reformation, bears a faithful testimony against Roman Catholicism and preaches in the way that men such as Jewell and Latimer used to preach he will probably be thought a firebrand and one who brings trouble on Israel, and told he is no friend of the church. But I can see plainly that they are not the most loyal friends of the church who talk the most loudly about supporting the church. I remember that none shouted 'Treason!' as loudly as Athaliah (2 Kings 11:14). Yet she was a traitor herself. I have observed that many who once talked the most about supporting the church have ended by forsaking the Church of England, and going over to Rome. Let men say what they will. The truest friends of the Church of England are those who labour most for the preservation of truth.

I lay these things before my readers, and invite their serious attention to them. I charge them never to forget that truth is of more importance to a church than peace. I ask them to be ready to carry out the principles I have laid down, and to contend earnestly, if necessary, for the truth. If we do this, we shall have learned something from Antioch.

3. There is no doctrine that we ought to guard so jealously as justification by faith

But I pass on to the third lesson from Antioch. That lesson is that there is no doctrine that we ought to guard so jealously as justification by faith without the deeds of the law.

The proof of this lesson stands out most prominently in the passage of Scripture quoted at the beginning of this chapter.

What one article of the faith had the apostle Peter denied at Antioch? None. What doctrine had he publicly preached which was false? None. What, then, had he done? He had done this: after once keeping company with the believing Gentiles as 'fellow heirs, of the same body, and partakers of his promise in Christ through the gospel' (Eph. 3:6), he suddenly became shy of them and withdrew himself. He seemed to think they were less holy and acceptable to God than the circumcised Jews. He seemed to imply that the believing Gentiles were in a lower state than those who had kept the ceremonies of the law of Moses. He seemed, in a word, to add something to simple faith as being necessary to give man an interest in Jesus Christ. He seemed to reply to the question, 'What must I do to be saved?' not merely, 'Believe on the Lord Jesus Christ,' but 'Believe on the Lord Jesus Christ and be circumcised and keep the ceremonies of the law.'

Such conduct as this the apostle Paul would not endure for a moment. Nothing so moved him as the idea of adding anything to the gospel of Christ. 'I withstood him,' he says, 'to his face.' He not only rebuked him, but he recorded the whole transaction fully when by inspiration of the Spirit he wrote the Epistle to the Galatians.

I invite special attention to this point. I ask men to observe the remarkable jealousy which the apostle Paul shows about this doctrine, and to consider the point about which such a stir was made. Let us note in this passage of Scripture the immense importance of justification by faith without the deeds of the law. Let us learn here what strong reasons the Reformers had for calling it (in the eleventh of the Thirty-nine Articles of the Church of England) 'a most wholesome doctrine and very full of comfort'.

Firstly, *this is the doctrine which is essentially necessary to our own personal comfort.* No one on earth is a real child of God, and a saved soul, till he sees and receives salvation by faith in Christ Jesus. No one will ever have solid peace and true assurance, until he embraces with all his heart the doctrine that we are counted as righteous before God because of the merit of our Lord Jesus Christ, by faith, and not for our own works or any merit in us. One reason, I believe, why so many who claim to be Christians are tossed to and fro, enjoy little comfort and feel little peace is their ignorance on this point. They do not see clearly justification by faith without the deeds of the law.

Secondly, *this is the doctrine which the great enemy of souls hates and labours to overthrow.* He knows that it turned the world upside down at the first beginning of the gospel in the days of the apostles. He knows that it turned the world upside down again at the time of the Reformation. He is therefore always tempting men to reject it. He is always trying to seduce churches and ministers to deny or obscure its truth. No wonder that the Council of Trent directed its chief attack against this doctrine, and pronounced it accursed and heretical. No wonder that many who think themselves learned in these days denounce the doctrine as theological jargon, and say that all people who take their religion seriously are justified by Christ, whether they have faith or not! The plain truth is that the doctrine is all bitterness and mortification to unconverted hearts. It just meets the needs of the awakened soul. But the proud man, who has never been humbled, who is not conscious of his own sin and does not see his own weakness, cannot receive its truth.

Thirdly, *this is the doctrine, the absence of which accounts for half the errors of the Roman Catholic Church.* The beginning of half the unscriptural doctrines of Roman Catholicism may be traced back to rejection of justification by faith. No Roman Catholic teacher, if he is faithful to his church, can say to an anxious sinner, 'Believe on the Lord Jesus Christ, and you will be saved.' He cannot do it without additions and explanations which completely destroy the good news. He dare not give the gospel medicine without adding something which destroys its effectiveness and neutralizes its power. Purgatory, penance, absolution from sin by a priest, the intercession of saints, the worship of the Virgin, and many other man-made services of Roman Catholicism all spring from this source. They are all rotten props to support weary consciences, but they are rendered necessary by the denial of justification by faith.

Fourthly, *this is the doctrine which is absolutely essential to a minister's success among his people.* Obscurity on this point spoils all. Absence of clear statements about justification will prevent even the most zealous minister from doing good. There may be much that is pleasing and attractive in a minister's sermons, much about Christ and mystical union with him, much about self-denial, much about humility, much about showing love to others. But all this will profit little, if his trumpet gives an uncertain sound about justification by faith without the deeds of the law.

Fifthly, *this is the doctrine which is absolutely essential to the prosperity of a church.* No church is really in a healthy state, in which this doctrine is not prominently brought forward. A church may have good forms of worship and regularly ordained ministers and the proper administration of the sacraments,[3] but a church will not see conversion of souls going on as a result of the message proclaimed from its pulpits when this doctrine is not plainly preached. Its schools may be found in every town and village. Its church buildings may strike the eye all over the land. But there will be no blessing from God on that church unless justification by faith is proclaimed from its pulpits. Sooner or later its lampstand will be taken away.

---

3. i.e. baptism and the Lord's Supper.

Why have the churches of Africa and the East fallen into such a sad state? Did they not have properly ordained ministers to oversee them? They had. Did they not have properly prescribed forms of worship? They had. Did they not have church synods and councils to make important decisions? They had. But they cast away the doctrine of justification by faith. They lost sight of that mighty truth, and so they fell.

Why did the Church of England do so little in the eighteenth century, and why did the Congregationalists and Methodists and Baptists do so much more? Was it that their system was better? No. Was it that the Anglican Church was not so well adapted to meet the requirements of lost souls? No. But their ministers preached justification by faith and the Anglican ministers, in too many cases, did not preach the doctrine at all.

Why do so many people in England continue to go to nonconformist churches? Why do we so often see a splendid Gothic parish church as empty of worshippers as a barn in July, and a little plain brick building, a chapel or gospel hall, filled so that there is scarcely room to breathe? Is it that people in general have any abstract dislike of bishops, the Prayer Book, clergymen wearing surplices or of the established church as such? Not at all! The simple reason is, in the vast majority of cases, that people do not like preaching in which justification by faith is not fully proclaimed. When they cannot hear it in their parish church they will seek it elsewhere. No doubt there are exceptions. No doubt there are places where a long course of neglect has thoroughly disgusted people with the Church of England, so that they will not even hear truth from its ministers. But I believe, as a general rule, when the parish church is empty and the meeting-hall is full, it will be found on enquiry that there is a cause.

If this is the case, the apostle Paul might well be jealous for the truth, and oppose Peter to his face. He might well maintain that anything ought to be sacrificed, rather than endanger the doctrine of justification in the church of Christ. He saw with a prophetical eye things that were to come. He left us all an example that we should do well to follow. Whatever we tolerate, let us never allow any injury to be done to that blessed doctrine — that we are justified by faith without the deeds of the law.

Let us always beware of any teaching which, either directly or indirectly, obscures justification by faith. All religious systems which put anything except simple faith between the sinner, labouring under the heavy burden of his sin, and Jesus Christ the Saviour, are dangerous and unscriptural. All systems which make faith out to be anything complicated, anything but a simple, childlike dependence — the hand which receives from the doctor the medicine for the soul — are unsafe and poisonous systems. All systems which cast discredit on the simple Protestant doctrine which broke the power of Roman Catholicism carry about with them a plague-spot and are dangerous to souls.

Baptism is a sacrament ordained by Christ himself and to be used with reverence and respect by all professing Christians. When it is used rightly, worthily and with faith, it is capable of being the instrument of mighty blessings to the soul. But when people are taught that *all* who are baptized are as a matter of course born again, and that *all* baptized persons should be addressed as 'children of God', I believe their souls are in great danger. Such teaching about baptism appears to me to overthrow the doctrine of justification by faith. Only those who have faith in Christ Jesus are children of God. And all men do *not* have faith.

The Lord's Supper is a sacrament ordained by Christ himself, and intended for the edification and refreshment of true believers. But when people are taught that all persons ought to come to the Lord's Table, whether they have faith or not, and that all alike receive Christ's body and blood who receive the bread and wine, I believe their souls are in great danger.

Such teaching appears to me to darken the doctrine of justification by faith. No one eats Christ's body and drinks Christ's blood except the one who is justified. And none are justified until they believe.

Membership of the Church of England is a great privilege. No visible church on earth, in my opinion, offers so many advantages to its members, when rightly administered. But when people are taught that because they are members of the church, they are as a matter of course members of Christ, I believe their souls are in great danger. Such teaching appears to me to overthrow the doctrine of justification by faith. Only those who believe are joined to Christ. And all men do *not* believe.

Whenever we hear teaching which obscures or contradicts justification by faith, we may be sure there is a screw loose somewhere. We should watch against such teaching, and be upon our guard. Once let a man go wrong about justification, and he will bid a long farewell to comfort, to peace, to a living hope, to anything like assurance in his Christianity. An error here is a worm gnawing at the root.

Words of advice to the reader

Seek to acquire a thorough knowledge of the Word of God

In conclusion, let me first of all ask everyone who reads this book to arm himself with a thorough knowledge of the written Word of God. Unless we do this we are at the mercy of any false teacher. We shall not see through the mistakes of an erring Peter. We shall not be able to imitate the faithfulness of a courageous Paul. An ignorant congregation will always be a source of nothing but trouble to a church. A Bible-reading congregation may save a church from ruin. Let us read the Bible regularly, daily and with fervent prayer, and become familiar with its contents. Let us receive nothing, believe nothing,

follow nothing which is not in the Bible, nor can be proved by
the Bible. Let our rule of faith, the touchstone of all our teaching, be the written Word of God.

A special appeal to members of the Anglican Church

In the next place, let me recommend to every member of the
Church of England that he make himself acquainted with the
Thirty-Nine Articles of his own church. (They are to be found
at the end of most Prayer Books.) They will abundantly repay
an attentive reading. They are the true standard by which loyalty to the church is to be tried, next to the Bible. They are the
test by which Anglicans should prove the teaching of their
ministers, if they want to know whether it is 'church teaching'
or not. I deeply lament the ignorance of systematic Christianity which prevails among many who attend the services of the
Church of England. It would be a good thing if such books as
Archbishop Usher's *Body of Divinity* were better known and
studied more than they are. If Dean Nowell's Catechism [the
catechism drawn up and approved by the body of men who
drew up the Thirty-Nine Articles] had ever been formally accredited as a means of teaching the doctrines of the Church of
England, many of the heresies which have crept into the church
could never have lived for a day. But unhappily many persons
really know no more about the true doctrines of the church of
which they are members than do followers of pagan religions
or of Islam. It is useless to expect the ordinary church members to be zealous for the maintenance of true doctrine, unless
they know what their own church has defined true doctrine to
be.

Be ready to contend earnestly for the faith

In the next place, let me entreat all who read this book to be
always ready to contend for the faith of Christ, if necessary. I

am not recommending that anyone should foster a controversial spirit. I do not want anyone to be like Goliath, going up and down saying, 'Give me a man to fight with.' Always feeding on controversy is poor work indeed. It is like feeding on bones. But I do say that no love of false peace should prevent us from contending jealously against false doctrine, and seeking to promote true doctrine, wherever we possibly can. True gospel in the pulpit, true gospel in the missionary societies we support, true gospel in the books we read, true gospel in the friends we associate with — let this be our aim, and never let us be ashamed to let men see that it is so.

Keep a careful watch on your own heart

In the next place, let me entreat all who read this paper to keep a jealous watch over their own hearts in these controversial times. There is much need of this caution. In the heat of the battle we are apt to forget our own inward man. Victory in argument is not always victory over the world or victory over the devil. Let the meekness of Peter in taking a reproof be as much our example as the boldness of Paul in reproving. Happy is the Christian who can call the person who faithfully rebukes him a 'beloved brother' (2 Peter 3:15). Let us strive to be holy in all our conduct, and not least in our tempers. Let us labour to maintain an uninterrupted communion with the Father and with the Son, and to keep up constant habits of private prayer and Bible-reading. In this way we shall be armed for the battle of life and have the sword of the Spirit well fitted to our hand when the day of temptation comes.

Pray regularly for the church

In the last place, let me entreat all church members who know what real praying is to pray daily for the church to which they belong. Let us pray that the Holy Spirit may be poured out upon it, and that its lampstand may not be taken away. Let us pray for those local churches in which the gospel is now not preached, that the darkness may pass away and the true light shine in them. Let us pray for those ministers who now neither know nor preach the truth, that God may take away the veil from their hearts and show them a more excellent way. Nothing is impossible. The apostle Paul was once a persecuting Pharisee; Luther was once an unenlightened monk; Bishop Latimer was once a bigoted supporter of Roman Catholicism; Thomas Scott was once thoroughly opposed to evangelical truth. Nothing, I repeat, is impossible. The Spirit can make ministers preach that gospel which they now labour to destroy. Let us therefore be urgent in prayer.

I commend the matters contained in this chapter to serious attention. Let us ponder them well in our hearts. Let us carry them out in our daily practice. Let us do this, and we shall have learned something from the story of Peter at Antioch.

7.
Apostolic fears

'I fear, lest somehow, as the serpent deceived Eve by his craftiness, so your minds may be corrupted from the simplicity that is in Christ' (2 Cor. 11:3).

The text which introduces this chapter contains one aspect of the experience of a very famous Christian. No servant of Christ, perhaps, has left such a mark for good on the world as the apostle Paul. When he was born the whole Roman Empire, except for one little corner, was sunk in the darkest heathenism; when he died the mighty fabric of heathenism was shaken to its very centre and ready to fall. And none of the agents whom God used to produce this marvellous change did more than Saul of Tarsus, after his conversion. Yet even in the midst of his successes and usefulness we find him crying out, 'I fear...'

There is a melancholy ring about these words which demands our attention. They show a man of many cares and anxieties. Anyone who supposes that Paul lived a life of ease, because he was a chosen apostle, worked miracles, founded churches and wrote inspired epistles, still has much to learn. Nothing can be further from the truth! The eleventh chapter of the Second Epistle to the Corinthians tells a very different tale. It is a chapter which deserves attentive study. Partly from the opposition of the heathen philosophers and priests, whose trade was in danger, partly from the bitter hostility of his own unbelieving countrymen, partly from false or weak brethren,

partly from his own thorn in the flesh — the great apostle of
the Gentiles was like his Master, 'a man of sorrows and
acquainted with grief' (Isa. 53:3).

But of all the burdens which Paul had to carry, none seems
to have weighed him down so much as that to which he refers
when he writes to the Corinthians of 'my deep concern for all
the churches' (2 Cor. 11:28). The scanty knowledge of many
of these early Christians, their weak faith, their shallow experience, their dim hope, their low standard of holiness — all these
things made them particularly liable to be led astray by false
teachers and to depart from the faith. Like little children, hardly
able to walk, they required to be treated with immense patience.
Like exotic plants in a hothouse, they had to be watched with
incessant care. Can we doubt that they kept their apostolic
founder in a state of constant tender anxiety? Can we wonder
that he says to the Colossians, '... what a great conflict I have
for you' (Col. 2:1) and to the Galatians, 'I marvel that you are
turning away so soon from him who called you in the grace of
Christ, to a different gospel.' 'O foolish Galatians! Who has
bewitched you...?' (Gal. 1:6; 3:1).

No attentive reader can study the epistles without seeing
this subject repeatedly cropping up. And the text quoted at
the beginning of this chapter is a sample of what I mean: 'I
fear, lest somehow, as the serpent deceived Eve by his craftiness, so your minds may be corrupted from the simplicity that
is in Christ.' That text contains three important lessons, which
I wish to press on the attention of all my readers. I believe in
my conscience they are lessons for the times.

1. First, the text shows us a spiritual disease to which
we are all susceptible, and which we ought to fear. That
disease is corruption of our minds: 'I fear, lest ... your
minds may be corrupted.'

2. Secondly, the text shows us an example which we ought to remember, as a beacon: 'The serpent deceived Eve by his craftiness.'

3. Thirdly, the text shows us a point about which we ought to be especially on our guard. That point is corruption 'from the simplicity that is in Christ'.

The text is a deep mine, and is not without difficulty. But let us go down into it boldly, and we shall find it contains much precious metal.

1. Corruption of our minds

First, then, there is a spiritual disease, which we ought to fear: corruption of our minds. I take 'corruption of our minds' to mean injury of our minds by the reception of false and unscriptural doctrines in religion. And I believe the apostle's meaning to be: 'I fear that your minds may be influenced by erroneous and unsound views of Christianity. I fear that you may come to accept as truths principles which are not the truth. I fear that you may depart from the faith once for all delivered to the saints, and embrace views which are in practice destructive of the gospel of Christ.'

The fear expressed by the apostle is painfully instructive, and at first sight may create surprise. Who would have thought that before the very eyes of Christ's own chosen disciples — while the blood of Calvary was hardly yet dry, while the age of miracles had not yet passed away — who would have thought that in a day like this there was any danger of Christians departing from the faith? Yet nothing is more certain than that 'the mystery of lawlessness' began already to work before the apostles were dead (2 Thess. 2:7). 'Even now,' says John, 'many antichrists have come' (1 John 2:18). And no fact in church history is more clearly proved than this — that false doctrine has never ceased to be the plague of Christendom for the last two thousand years. Looking forward with the eye of a prophet, Paul might well say, 'I fear...' — 'I fear, not merely the corruption of your morals, but of your minds.'

The plain truth is that *false doctrine* has been the chosen device which Satan has employed in every age to stop the progress of the gospel of Christ. Finding himself unable to prevent the fountain of life being opened, he has laboured incessantly to poison the streams which flow from it. If he could not destroy it, he has too often neutralized its usefulness by addition, subtraction, or substitution. In a word, he has 'corrupted' men's minds.

False doctrine soon spread throughout *the early church* after the death of the apostles, whatever some people may say about the purity of the early church. Partly by strange teaching about the Trinity and the person of Christ, partly by an absurd multiplication of newfangled rituals, partly by the introduction of monasticism and a man-made asceticism, the light of the church was soon dimmed and its usefulness destroyed. Even in Augustine's time, as the preface to the English Prayer Book tells us, rituals had become so numerous that Christian people were in a worse state concerning this matter than were the Jews. Here was the corruption of men's minds.

False doctrine in *the Middle Ages* so completely spread throughout the church that the truth as it is in Jesus was almost completely buried or drowned. During the last three centuries before the Reformation, it is probable that very few Christians in Europe could have answered the question: 'What must I do to be saved?' Popes and cardinals, abbots and priors, archbishops and bishops, priests and deacons, monks and nuns were, with a few rare exceptions, steeped in ignorance and superstition. They were sunk into a deep sleep, from which they were only partially roused by the earthquake of the Reformation. Here, again, was the corruption of men's minds.

False doctrine, *since the days of the Reformation*, has continually been rising up again, and marring the work which the Reformers began. A reversion to Rome in some districts of Europe, denial of the Trinity and the miraculous in others, mere formal religion and apathy in others have withered blossoms which once promised to bear good fruit, and made Protestantism a mere barren form. Here, again, has been the 'corruption of the mind'.

False doctrine, even in our own day and before our own eyes, is eating out the heart of the Church of England and endangering her existence. One party within the church does not hesitate to avow its dislike to the principles of the Reformation, and travels land and sea to turn the established church into a Roman Catholic organization. Another party, with equal boldness, speaks lightly of inspiration, sneers at the very idea of a supernatural religion and tries hard to cast overboard miracles as so many useless encumbrances. Another party proclaims liberty to every shade and form of religious opinion, and tells us that all teachers are equally deserving of our confidence, however diverse and contradictory their opinions, if only they are clever, earnest and sincere. To each and to all the same remark applies. They illustrate the 'corruption of men's minds'.

In the face of such facts as these, we may well take to heart the words of the apostle in the text which introduces this chapter. Like him we have ample cause to feel afraid. Never, I think, was there such need for Christians in this land to stand on their guard. Never was there such need for faithful ministers to speak out boldly, holding nothing back. 'If the trumpet makes an uncertain sound, who will prepare himself for battle?' (1 Cor. 14:8).

I charge every loyal member of the Church of England to open his eyes to the peril in which his own church stands, and to beware lest it suffer damage through apathy and a morbid love of peace. Controversy is an odious thing, but there are times when it is a positive duty. Peace is an excellent thing but, like gold, it may be bought at too high a price. Unity is a mighty blessing, but it is worthless if it is purchased at the cost of truth. Once more I say, 'Open your eyes and be on your guard.'

The nation that rests satisfied with its commercial prosperity and neglects its national defences, because they are troublesome or expensive, is likely to become a prey to the first aggressor, such as Attila the Hun or Napoleon, who chooses to attack it. The church which is 'rich' and has 'become wealthy' may think it has 'need of nothing' because of its antiquity, traditions and endowments. It may cry, 'Peace, peace,' and flatter itself that it will see no evil befall it. But if it is not careful about the maintenance of sound doctrine among its ministers and members, it must never be surprised if its lampstand is taken away.

I deplore, from the bottom of my heart, despondency or cowardice in the face of this crisis. All I say is, let us exercise a godly fear. I do not see the slightest necessity for forsaking the old ship, and giving it up for lost. Bad as things look inside our ark, they are no better outside. But I do protest against that careless spirit of slumber which seems to seal the eyes of many in the church, and to blind them to the enormous peril in which we are placed by the rise and progress of false doctrine in these days. I protest against the common notion, so often proclaimed by men in high places, that unity is of more importance than sound doctrine, and peace more valuable than truth. And I call on every reader who really loves the Church of England to recognize the dangers of the times and to do his duty, courageously and energetically, in resisting them by united action and by prayer. It was not for nothing that our Lord said, 'He who has no sword, let him sell his garment and buy one' (Luke 22:36). Let us not forget Paul's words: 'Watch, stand fast in the faith, be brave, be strong' (1 Cor. 16:13). Our noble Reformers bought the truth at the price of their own blood, and handed it down to us. Let us take care that we do not stoop so low as to sell our birthright for the sake of so-called unity and peace.

2. Deception by the craftiness of the devil

Secondly, the text shows us an example we would do well to remember, as a beacon: 'The serpent deceived Eve by his craftiness.' I need hardly remind my readers that Paul here refers to the story of the Fall in the third chapter of Genesis as a simple historical fact. He does not give the slightest degree of support to the modern notion that the book of Genesis is nothing more than a pleasing collection of myths and fables. He does not hint that there is no such being as the devil, and that there was not any literal eating of the forbidden fruit, and that it was not really in this way that sin entered into the world. On the contrary, he narrates the story of the third chapter of Genesis as a trustworthy account of something that really took place.

You should also remember that this reference to the early chapters of the Bible does not stand alone. It is a noteworthy fact that several of the most remarkable histories and miracles of the Pentateuch are expressly mentioned in the New Testament, and always as historical facts. Cain and Abel, Noah's ark, the destruction of Sodom, Esau's selling his birthright, the destruction of the first-born in Egypt, the crossing of the Red Sea, the serpent of brass, the manna, the water flowing from the rock, Balaam's donkey speaking — all these things are named by the writers of the New Testament, and named as matters of fact, and not as fables. Let that never be forgotten. Those who are fond of pouring contempt on Old Testament miracles, and making light of the authority of the Pentateuch, would do well to consider whether they know better than our Lord Jesus Christ and the apostles.

To my mind, to talk of Genesis as a collection of myths and fables, in the face of such a text of Scripture as we have before us in this chapter, sounds both unreasonable and profane. Was Paul mistaken or not, when he narrated the story of the temptation and the Fall? If he was, he was a weak-minded, gullible person and may have been mistaken on fifty other subjects. At this rate there is an end to all his authority as a writer! From such a monstrous conclusion we may well turn away with scorn. But it is well to remember that open unbelief often begins with irreverent contempt of the Old Testament.

The point, after all, which the apostle would have us take note of in the account of Eve's fall, is the 'craftiness', or subtlety, with which the devil led her into sin. He did not tell her flatly that he wished to deceive her and do her harm. On the contrary, he told her that the thing forbidden was a thing that was 'good for food' and 'pleasant to the eyes, and ... desirable to make one wise' (Gen. 3:6). He had no scruples about asserting that she could eat the forbidden fruit and yet 'not die'. He blinded her eyes to the sinfulness and danger of breaking God's law. He persuaded her to believe that to depart from God's plain command was for her benefit and not for her ruin. In short, 'he deceived her by his craftiness'.

Now this 'craftiness', Paul tells us, is precisely what we have to fear in false doctrine. We are not to expect it to approach our minds in the garb of error, but in the form of truth. Counterfeit money would never pass into circulation if it did not appear like the real thing. The wolf would seldom get into the fold if he did not enter it in sheep's clothing. Roman Catholicism and downright unbelief would do little harm if they went about the world under their true names. Satan is far too wise a general to manage a campaign in such a manner as this. He employs fine words and high-sounding phrases, such as 'universally accepted', 'apostolic tradition', 'unity', 'church order', 'sound church views', 'freedom of thought', 'broadmindedness', 'charitable judgement', 'liberal interpretation of Scripture', and the like, and thus secures a foothold in the minds of the unwary. And this is precisely the 'craftiness' which Paul refers to in the text. We need not doubt that he had read his Master's solemn words in the Sermon on the Mount: 'Beware of false prophets, who come to you in sheep's clothing, but inwardly they are ravenous wolves' (Matt. 7:15).

I ask you to pay special attention to this point. Such is the simplicity and innocence of many in the church today, that they actually expect false doctrine to look false, and will not understand that, as a rule, the very essence of its ability to do harm is its resemblance to God's truth.

A young clergyman, for instance, brought up from his cradle to hear nothing but evangelical teaching, is suddenly invited some day to hear a sermon preached by some eminent teacher whose opinions lean towards Roman Catholicism or scepticism. He goes into the church, expecting in his simplicity to hear nothing but heresy from beginning to end. To his amazement he hears a clever, eloquent sermon, containing a vast amount of truth, with only a few insidious drops of error added. Too often a violent reaction takes place in his simple, innocent, unsuspecting mind. He begins to think his former teachers were bigoted, narrow-minded and uncharitable, and his confidence in them is shaken, perhaps for ever. Too often, sadly, it ends with his being led completely astray and at last he is enrolled in the ranks of the ritualists or the liberals! And what lies at the root of all that happens to him? A foolish forgetfulness of the lesson Paul puts forward in this text. 'As the serpent deceived Eve by his craftiness,' so Satan deceives unwary souls in our day by approaching them under the garb of truth.

I entreat every reader of this book to remember this particular point, and to stand on his guard. What is more common than to hear it said of some false teacher in this day and age: 'He is so good, so devoted, so kind, so zealous, so hardworking, so humble, so self-denying, so charitable, so earnest, so fervent, so clever, so evidently sincere, there can be no danger and no harm in hearing him. Besides, he preaches so much of the real gospel; no one can preach a better sermon than he does sometimes! I never can, and never will, believe he is not sound'? Who does not continually hear such talk as this? What discerning eye can fail to see that many in the church expect unsound teachers to be openly disseminating poison, and cannot realize that such teachers often appear as 'angels of light', and are far too wise to be always saying all they think and showing their whole hand and mind. But so it is. Never was it so necessary to remember the words: 'The serpent deceived Eve by his craftiness.'

I leave this point with the sorrowful remark that we live in times when suspicion on the subject of sound doctrine is not only a duty but a virtue. It is not the openly avowed Pharisee and Sadducee that we have to fear, but the *leaven* of the Pharisees and Sadducees. It is the 'appearance of wisdom' with which ritualism is invested that makes it so dangerous to many minds (Col. 2:23). It seems so good and fair and zealous and holy and reverent and devout and kind that it carries away many well-meaning people like a flood. He that would be safe must cultivate the spirit of a sentinel at a critical post. He must not mind being laughed at and ridiculed, as someone who 'has a keen nose for heresy'. In days like these he must not be ashamed to suspect danger. And if anyone scoffs at him for doing so, he may well be content to reply, 'The serpent deceived Eve by his craftiness.'

3. The simplicity that is in Christ

The third and last lesson of the text remains yet to be considered. It shows us a point about which we ought to be especially on our guard. That point is called 'the simplicity that is in Christ'. Now this expression is somewhat remarkable and stands alone in the New Testament. One thing, at any rate, is abundantly clear: the word 'simplicity' means that which is single and unmixed, by way of contrast to that which is mixed and double. Following out that idea, some have held that the expression means 'singleness of affection towards Christ'; we are to fear lest we should divide our affections between Christ and any other. This is no doubt very good theology, but I question whether it is the true sense of the text. I prefer the opinion that the expression means the simple, unmixed, unadulterated, unaltered doctrine of Christ — the simple 'truth as it is in Jesus' on all points — without addition, subtraction, or substitution. Departure from the simple, genuine prescription of the gospel, either by leaving out any part or adding any part, was the thing Paul would have the Corinthians dread more than any other. The expression is full of meaning and seems especially written for our learning in these last days. We are to be always jealously on our guard, lest we depart from and corrupt the simple gospel which Christ once delivered to the saints.

The expression we are considering is exceedingly instructive. The principle it contains is of unspeakable importance. If we love our souls and would keep them in a healthy state, we must endeavour to adhere closely to the simple doctrine of

Christ, down to the smallest detail and in every particular. Once add to it, or take away anything from it, and you risk spoiling the divine medicine, and may even turn it into poison. Let your ruling principle be: 'No other doctrine but that of Christ — nothing less and nothing more!' Lay firm hold on that principle, and never let it go. Write it on the tablet of your heart (2 Cor. 3:3), and never forget it.

Let us settle it, for example, firmly in our minds that there is no *way of peace* but the simple way marked out by Christ. True rest of conscience and inward peace of soul will never come from anything but direct faith in Christ himself and his finished work. Peace by confession to a priest, or bodily asceticism, or incessant attendance at church services, or frequent reception of the Lord's Supper, is a delusion and a snare. It is only by coming straight to Jesus himself, labouring and heavy laden, and by believing, trusting communion with him, that souls find rest. In this matter let us stand fast in 'the simplicity that is in Christ'.

Let us settle it next in our minds that there is no other *priest* who can be in any way a mediator between yourself and God but Jesus Christ. He himself has said — and his word shall not pass away — 'No one comes to the Father except through me' (John 14:6). No sinful child of Adam, whatever his ministerial qualifications, and however high his ecclesiastical title, can ever occupy Christ's place, or do what Christ alone is appointed to do. The priesthood is Christ's own special office, and it is one which he has never delegated to another. In this matter also let us stand fast in 'the simplicity that is in Christ'.

Let us settle it next in our minds that there is no *sacrifice for sin* except the one sacrifice of Christ upon the cross. Do not listen for a moment to those who tell you that there is any sacrifice in the Lord's Supper, any repetition of Christ's offering on the cross, or any offering up of his body and blood to God, under the form of consecrated bread and wine. The one sacrifice for sins which Christ offered was a perfect and complete sacrifice, and it is nothing short of blasphemy to attempt to repeat it. 'By one offering he has perfected for ever those who are being sanctified' (Heb. 10:14). In this matter also let us stand fast in 'the simplicity that is in Christ'.

Let us settle it next in our minds that there is no other *rule of faith and judge of controversial matters* but that simple one to which Christ always referred — the written Word of God. Let no one disturb our souls by such vague expressions as 'the voice of the church', 'the earliest traditions', 'the judgement of the early Church Fathers', and similar tall talk. Let our only standard of truth be the Bible, God's written Word. 'What does the Scripture say?' (Rom. 4:3). 'What is written?' (Luke 10:26). 'To the law and to the testimony!' (Isa. 8:20). 'Search the Scriptures' (John 5:39, AV). In this matter also let us stand fast in 'the simplicity that is in Christ'.

Let us settle it next in our minds that there are no other *means of grace* in the church which have any binding authority, except those well-known and simple ones which Christ and the apostles have sanctioned. Let us regard with a jealous suspicion all ceremonies and forms of man's invention, when they are invested with such exaggerated importance as to thrust into the background God's own appointments. It is the invariable tendency of man's inventions to supersede God's ordinances. Let us beware of making the Word of God of none effect by human devices. In this matter also let us stand fast in 'the simplicity that is in Christ'.

Let us settle it next in our minds that no teaching about *the sacraments* is sound which gives them a power of which Christ says nothing. Let us beware of admitting that either baptism or the Lord's Supper can confer grace by their mere outward administration, independently of the state of heart of those who receive them. Let us remember that the only proof that baptized people and communicants have grace is the exhibition of grace in their lives. The fruits of the Spirit are the only evidences that we are born of the Spirit and one with Christ, and not the mere fact of receiving the sacraments. In this matter also let us stand fast in 'the simplicity that is in Christ'.

Let us settle it next in our minds that no teaching about *the Holy Spirit* is safe which cannot be reconciled with the simple teaching of Christ. Those who assert that the Holy Spirit actually dwells in all baptized people, without exception, by virtue of their baptism, and that this grace within such people only needs to be 'stirred up', are not to be given a hearing. The simple teaching of our Lord is that he dwells only in those who are his believing disciples, and that the world neither knows, nor sees, nor can receive the Holy Spirit (John 14:17). His indwelling is the special privilege of Christ's people and where he is, he will be seen. On this point also let us stand fast in 'the simplicity that is in Christ'.

Finally let us settle it in our minds that no teaching can be thoroughly sound, in which truth is not set forth in *the same proportions as in the teaching of Christ and the apostles*. Let us beware of any teaching in which the main thing is an incessant exaltation of the church, the ministry, or the sacraments, while such grand truths as repentance, faith, conversion and holiness are left in a comparatively subordinate and inferior place. Place such teaching side by side with the teaching of the Gospels, Acts and epistles. Count up texts. Make a calculation. Note how *comparatively* little is said in the New Testament about baptism, the Lord's Supper, the church and the ministry; and then judge for yourself what is the proportion of truth. In this matter also, I say once more, let us stand fast in 'the simplicity that is in Christ'.

The simple doctrine and rule of Christ, then — nothing added, nothing taken away, nothing substituted — this is the mark at which we ought to aim. This is the point from which departure ought to be dreaded. Can we improve on his

teaching? Are we wiser than he? Can we suppose that he left
anything of real, vital importance unwritten, or subject to the
vague reports of human traditions? Shall we take on ourselves
to say that we can mend or change for the better any ordi-
nance that he has appointed? Can we doubt that in matters
about which he is silent we need to act very cautiously, very
gently, very moderately, and must beware of pressing them on
those who do not see with our eyes? Above all, must we not
beware of asserting anything to be necessary for salvation if
Christ has said nothing at all about it? I only see one answer to
such questions as these. We must beware of anything which
has even the appearance of departure from 'the simplicity that
is in Christ'.

The plain truth is that we cannot sufficiently exalt the Lord
Jesus Christ as the great Head of the church, and Lord of all
ordinances, no less than as the Saviour of sinners. I take it we
all fail here. We do not realize how high and great and glorious a King the Son of God is, and what undivided loyalty we
owe to one who has not delegated any of his offices, or given
his glory to another. The solemn words which John Owen
addressed to the House of Commons, in a sermon on the 'great-
ness of Christ', deserve to be remembered. I fear the House of
Commons hears few such sermons in the present day.

Christ is the way; men without him are Cains, wan-
derers, vagabonds. His is the truth; men without him are
liars, like the devil of old. He is the life; men without
him are dead in trespasses and sins. He is the light; men
without him are in darkness, and do not know where
they are going. He is the vine; men that are not in him
are withered branches prepared for the fire. He is the
rock; men not built on him are carried away with a flood.
He is the Alpha and Omega, the first and the last, the
author and the end, the founder and finisher of our

salvation. The one who does not have him neither has the beginning of good nor will have the end of misery. Oh, blessed Jesus, how much better it would be not to exist than to live without you, never to be born than not to die in you! A thousand hells do not compare with what it means eternally to be without Jesus Christ.

This witness is true. If we can say 'Amen' to the spirit of this passage it will be well with our souls.

Advice to the reader

And now let me conclude this chapter by offering a few parting words of counsel to any who may read this book. I offer them not as one who has any authority, but as one who affectionately desires to do good to his brethren. I offer them especially to all who are members of the Church of England, though I believe they will be found useful by all Christians. And I offer them as counsels which I find helpful to my own soul, and as such I venture to think they will be helpful to others.

Study the Scriptures thoroughly

In the first place, if we would be kept from falling away into false doctrine, let us arm our minds with a thorough knowledge of God's Word. Let us read our Bibles from beginning to end with daily diligence and constant prayer for the teaching of the Holy Spirit, and so strive to become thoroughly familiar with their contents. Ignorance of the Bible is the root of all error, and a superficial acquaintance with it accounts for many of the sad perversions and defections of the present day. In an age of fast travel and easy means of communication, when everyone is constantly in a hurry, I am firmly persuaded that many Christians do not give enough time to private reading of the Scriptures. I am very doubtful whether people in England know their Bibles as well today as they did three hundred years ago. The consequence is that they are 'tossed to and fro and carried about with every wind of doctrine', and fall an easy prey to the first clever teacher of error who tries to influence their minds. I entreat my readers to remember this counsel, and keep a careful watch on their ways.

It is as true now as ever that the man who is thoroughly versed in the biblical text is the only good theologian, and that a familiarity with the great key passages of Scripture is, as our Lord proved in the temptation, one of the best safeguards against error. Arm yourself, then, with the sword of the Spirit, and let your hand become used to wielding it. I am well aware that there is no royal highway to Bible knowledge. Without diligence and taking pains no one ever becomes 'mighty in the Scriptures'. 'Justification,' said Charles Simeon, in his characteristically quaint manner, 'is by faith, but knowledge of the Bible comes by works.' But of one thing I am certain: there is no labour which will be so richly repaid as laborious regular daily study of God's Word.

Make yourself familiar with your church's confession of faith

In the second place [and here I especially address fellow-members of the Anglican Church], if we would keep a straight path as loyal members of the church in this evil day, let us be thoroughly acquainted with the Thirty-Nine Articles. Those articles, I am bold to say, are the authorized confession of faith of the Church of England and the true test by which the teaching of every clergyman ought to be tried.

The 'teaching of the Prayer Book' is a phrase commonly quoted and the Prayer Book is often held up as a better standard of what the church teaches than the articles. But I venture to assert that the articles, and not the Prayer Book, are the church's standard of church doctrine. Let no one suppose that I think lightly of the Prayer Book because I say this. In loyal love to the liturgy, and deep admiration of its contents, I give place to no man. Taken all in all, it is an incomparable book of devotion for the use of a Christian congregation. But the church's prayer book was never meant to be the church's fixed standard of Bible doctrine, in the same way that the articles are. This was not meant to be its role; this was not the purpose for which it was compiled. It is a manual of devotion; it is not a confession of faith. Let us value it highly, but let us not exalt it to the place which the articles alone can fill and which common sense, statute law and the express opinion of eminent theologians agree in assigning to them.

I entreat every reader [who is a member of the Anglican Church] to search the articles and to keep up familiar acquaintance with them by reading them carefully at least once a year. Settle it in your mind that no man has a right to call himself a loyal member of the church who preaches, teaches, or maintains anything contrary to the church's confession of faith. I believe the articles are unduly neglected. I think it would be well if in all schools connected with the Church of England they formed a part of the regular system of religious instruction. Like the famous Westminster Confession of Faith, they would be found to be a mighty barrier against the tendency to return to Rome.

Make yourself acquainted with the history of the Reformation period

The third and last piece of advice which I venture to offer is this: let us make ourselves thoroughly acquainted with the history of the Reformation. My reason for offering this counsel is my firm conviction that this highly important part of our history has of recent years been undeservedly neglected. Thousands of church members nowadays have a most inadequate notion of the amount of our debt to our martyred Reformers. They have no distinct conception of the state of darkness and superstition in which our fathers lived, and of the light and liberty which the Reformation brought in. And the consequence is that they see no great harm in the movement towards Rome in the present day, and have very indistinct ideas of the real nature and work of Roman Catholicism. It is high time that a better state of things should begin. Of one thing I am thoroughly convinced: a vast amount of the prevailing apathy about the trend towards Rome may be traced up to gross ignorance, both of the nature of Roman Catholicism and of the Protestant Reformation.

Ignorance, after all, is one of the best friends of false doctrine. More light is one of the great needs of the day. Thousands are led astray by Roman Catholicism or unbelief through sheer lack of reading and information. Once more, I repeat, if men would only study with attention the Bible, the old confessions of faith and the history of the Reformation, I should have little fear of their minds being 'corrupted from the simplicity that is in Christ'.

8.
Idolatry

'Flee from idolatry' (1 Cor. 10:14).

The text quoted at the head of this page may seem at first sight to be hardly needed in our land. In an age of education and intelligence like this, we might almost fancy it is a waste of time to tell anyone in this country to 'flee from idolatry'.

I am bold to say that this is a great mistake. I believe that we have come to a time when the subject of idolatry demands a thorough and searching investigation. I believe that idolatry is near us and around us and in the midst of us to a very fearful extent. The second commandment, in one word, is in danger. 'The plague has begun.' Without further preface, I propose in this chapter to consider the following four points:

1. The definition of idolatry. What is it?
2. The cause of idolatry. Where does it come from?
3. The form idolatry assumes in the visible church of Christ. Where is it?
4. The ultimate termination of idolatry. What will bring it to an end?

I feel that the subject is surrounded with many difficulties. Our lot is cast in an age when truth is constantly in danger of being sacrificed to what are wrongly called 'tolerance', 'love' and 'peace'. Nevertheless, I cannot forget, as a clergyman, that the church to which I belong is one which has in the past given clear warnings on the subject of idolatry and, unless I am greatly mistaken, truth about idolatry is, in the highest sense, truth for the times.

1. What is idolatry?

Let me, then, first of all supply a definition of idolatry. Let me show what it is. It is of the utmost importance that we should understand this. Unless I make this clear, I can do nothing with the subject. Vagueness and uncertainty about what is meant prevail upon this point, as upon almost every other in religion. The Christian who would not be continually running aground in his spiritual voyage must have his route clearly marked with warning buoys and his mind well stored with clear definitions.

I say then, that idolatry is a worship in which the honour due to God in Trinity, and to him only, is given to some of his creatures, or to some invention of his creatures. It may vary widely. It may assume different forms, according to the ignorance or the knowledge, the civilization or the barbarism, of those who offer it. It may be grossly absurd and ludicrous, or it may closely border on truth, and be capable of being defended in ways that appear most plausible. But whether in the adoration of the idol of Juggernaut, or in the adoration of the host [i.e. the consecrated bread used in the mass] in St Peter's at Rome, the principle of idolatry is in reality the same. In either case the honour due to God is turned aside from him and bestowed on that which is not God. And whenever this is done, whether in heathen temples or in professedly Christian churches, there is an act of idolatry.

It is not necessary for a man formally to deny God and Christ, in order to be an idolater. Far from it. Professed reverence for the God of the Bible and actual idolatry are perfectly compatible. They have often gone side by side, and they still do so.

The Israelites never thought of renouncing God when they persuaded Aaron to make the golden calf. 'This is your god,' they said (using the Hebrew word Elohim which is mainly used in the Old Testament as a name for the true God), 'that brought you out of the land of Egypt.' And the feast in honour of the calf was kept as a 'feast to the LORD' (that is, to Jehovah) (Exod. 32:4,5).

Jeroboam, to quote another example, never pretended to ask the ten tribes to cast off their allegiance to the God of David and Solomon. When he set up the calves of gold in Dan and Bethel he only said, 'It is too much for you to go up to Jerusalem. Here are your gods, O Israel, which brought you up from the land of Egypt' (1 Kings 12:28).

In both instances, we should observe, the idol was not set up as a rival to God, but under the pretence of being a help — a stepping-stone to his service. But in both instances a great sin was committed. The honour due to God was given to a visible representation of him. The majesty of Jehovah was offended. The second commandment was broken. There was, in the eyes of God, a flagrant act of idolatry.

Let us take careful note of this. It is high time to dismiss from our minds those loose ideas about idolatry which are common in this day. We must not think, as many do, that there are only two sorts of idolatry — the spiritual idolatry of the man who loves his wife, or child, or money more than God; and the open, gross idolatry of the man who bows down to an image of wood, or metal, or stone, because he knows no better. We may rest assured that idolatry is a sin which occupies a far wider field than this. It is not merely a thing that we may hear of in the Indian sub-continent and pity at missionary meetings; nor yet is it a thing confined to our own hearts, that we

may confess before the mercy-seat on our knees. It is a pestilence that walks in the church of Christ to a much greater
extent than many suppose. It is an evil that, like the man of sin,
'sits as God in the temple of God' (2 Thess. 2:4). It is a sin
that we all need to watch and pray against continually. It creeps
into our religious worship unnoticed, and is upon us before
we are aware. Those are tremendous words which Isaiah spoke
to the Jew who observed the outward forms of Old Testament
worship — not to the worshipper of Baal, remember, but to
the man who actually came to the temple:

> He who kills a bull is as if he slays a man;
> He who sacrifices a lamb, as if he breaks a dog's neck;
> He who offers a grain offering, as if he offers swine's
>   blood;
> He who burns incense, as if he blesses an idol
>   (Isa. 66:3).

This is the sin which God has especially denounced in his
Word. One commandment out of ten is devoted to the prohi-
bition of it. Not one of all the ten contains such a solemn declaration of God's character, and of his judgements against the
disobedient: 'I, the LORD your God, am a jealous God, visiting
the iniquity of the fathers on the children to the third and fourth
generations of those who hate me' (Exod. 20:5). Not one,
perhaps, of all the ten is so emphatically repeated and ampli-
fied, and especially in the fourth chapter of the book of
Deuteronomy.

This is the sin, of all others, to which the Jews seem to have
been most inclined before the destruction of Solomon's temple.
What is the history of Israel under their judges and kings but a
dismal record of repeated falling away into idolatry? Again
and again we read of 'high places' and false gods. Again and
again we read of captivities and chastisements on account of

idolatry. Again and again we read of a return to the old sin. It seems as if the love of idols among the Jews was naturally bone of their bone and flesh of their flesh. The besetting sin of the Old Testament church, in one word, was idolatry. In the face of the most elaborate ceremonial ordinances that God ever gave to his people, Israel was incessantly turning aside after idols and worshipping the work of men's hands.

This is the sin, of all others, which has brought down the heaviest judgements on the visible church. It brought on Israel the armies of Egypt, Assyria and Babylon. It scattered the ten tribes, burned up Jerusalem and carried Judah and Benjamin into captivity. It brought on the Eastern churches, in later days, the overwhelming flood of the Saracen invasion, and turned many a spiritual garden into a wilderness. The desolation which reigns where Cyprian and Augustine once preached, the living death in which the churches of Asia Minor and Syria are buried, are all attributable to this sin. All testify to the same great truth which the Lord proclaims in Isaiah: 'My glory I will not give to another' (Isa. 42:8).

Let us gather up these things in our minds, and ponder them well. Idolatry is a subject which, in every church of Christ that would keep herself pure, should be thoroughly examined, understood and known. It is not for nothing that Paul lays down the stern command: 'Flee from idolatry.'

2. Where does idolatry come from?

Let me show, in the second place, the cause to which idolatry may be traced. Where does it come from?

To the man who takes an extravagant and exalted view of human intellect and reason, idolatry may seem absurd. He imagines it is too irrational for any but weak minds to be endangered by it.

To a mere superficial thinker about Christianity, the dangers involved in idolatry may seem very small. Whatever commandments are broken, such a man will tell us, professing Christians are not very likely to violate the second.

Now, both these persons betray a woeful ignorance of human nature. They do not see that there are secret roots of idolatry within us all. The prevalence of idolatry in all ages among the heathen must necessarily puzzle the one; the warnings of Protestant ministers against idolatry in the church must necessarily appear uncalled for to the other. Both are alike blind to its cause.

The cause of all idolatry is *the natural corruption of man's heart*. That great family disease, with which all the children of Adam are infected from their birth, shows itself in this, as it does in a thousand other ways. Out of the same fountain from which 'proceed evil thoughts, adulteries, fornications, murders, thefts, covetousness, wickedness, deceit' and the like (Mark 7:21, 22) — out of that same fountain arise false views of God, and false views of the worship due to him and, therefore, when the apostle Paul tells the Galatians what the 'works of the flesh' are, he places prominently among them 'idolatry' (Gal. 5:20).

Man will always have a religion of some kind. God has not left himself without a witness in us all, fallen as we are. Like old inscriptions hidden under mounds of rubbish, like the almost-obliterated original writing in palimpsest manuscripts,[1] in just the same way there is a dim something engraved at the bottom of man's heart, however faint and half-erased — a something which makes him feel he must have a religion and a

---

1. 'Palimpsest' is the name given to ancient parchment manuscripts which have been written over twice — that is, the work of a comparatively modern writer has been written over, or across, the work of an older writer. Before the invention of cheap paper, the practice of writing over an old manuscript in this way was not uncommon. The object of the practice was, of course, to save expense. Unfortunately, the second writing was often far less valuable that the first.

worship of some kind. The proof of this is to be found in the history of voyages and travels in every part of the globe. The exceptions to the rule are so few, if indeed there are any, that they only confirm its truth. Man's worship in some dark corner of the earth may rise no higher than a vague fear of an evil spirit, and a desire to placate him, but a worship of some kind man will have.

But then comes in the effect of the Fall. Ignorance of God, natural and low conceptions of his nature and attributes, earthly and sensual notions of the service which is acceptable to him, all characterize the religion of the natural man. There is a craving in his mind after something in the divine being that he worships that he can see and feel and touch. He is eager to bring his God down to his own crawling level. He would make his religion a thing of sense and sight. He has no idea of the religion of heart and faith and spirit. In short, just as he is willing to live on God's earth but, until renewed by grace, to lead a fallen and degraded life, so he has no objection to worship after a fashion, but, until renewed by the Holy Spirit, it is always with a fallen worship. In one word, idolatry is a natural product of man's heart. It is a weed which, like the uncultivated earth, the heart is always ready to bring forth.

And now does it surprise us when we read of the constantly recurring idolatries of the Old Testament church — of Peor and Baal and Moloch and Chemosh and Ashtaroth, of high places and hill altars, and groves and images — and this in the full light of the ceremonial laid down by Moses? Let us no longer be surprised. It can be accounted for. There is a cause.

Does it surprise us when we read in history how idolatry crept in by degrees into the church of Christ, how little by little it thrust out gospel truth until, in Canterbury, men offered more at the shrine of Thomas à Becket than they did at the shrine of the Virgin Mary, and more at the shrine of Virgin Mary than at the one consecrated to Christ? Let us no longer be surprised. It is all intelligible. There is a cause.

Does it surprise us when we hear of men going over from
Protestant churches to the Roman Catholic Church, in the
present day? Do we find it hard to account for, and feel as if
we ourselves could never forsake a pure form of worship for
one like that represented by the pope? Let us no longer be
surprised. There is a solution for the problem. There is a cause.

That cause is nothing else but the corruption of man's heart.
There is a natural proneness and tendency in us all to give
God a worship that appeals to our senses and to the flesh, and
not that which is commanded in his Word. We are ever ready,
by reason of our laziness and unbelief, to devise visible helps
and stepping-stones in our approaches to him, and ultimately
to give these inventions of our own the honour due to him. In
fact, idolatry is all natural, downhill, easy, like the broad way.
Spiritual worship is all of grace, all uphill and all against the
grain. Any form of worship at all is more pleasing to the natural heart than worshipping God in the way which our Lord
Christ describes, 'in spirit and truth' (John 4:23).

I, for one, am not surprised at the quantity of idolatry exist-
ing, both in the world and in the visible church. I believe it
perfectly possible that we may yet live to see far more of it
than some have ever dreamed of. It would never surprise me if
some mighty personal Antichrist were to arise before the end
— mighty in intellect, mighty in talents for government, yes,
and mighty, *perhaps,* in miraculous gifts too. It would never
surprise me to see one such as I have described setting himself
up in opposition to Christ, and forming a conspiracy of unbelief
against the gospel. I believe that many would rejoice to do
him honour who now take pride in saying, 'We will not have
this Christ to reign over us.' I believe that many would make a
god of him and reverence him as an incarnation of truth and
concentrate their idea of hero-worship on his person. I ad-
vance it as a *possibility*, and no more. But of this at least I am
certain, that no man is less safe from the danger of idolatry

than the man who now sneers at every form of religion, and
that from unbelief to gullibility, from atheism to the worst types
of idolatry, there is but a single step.

Let us not think, in any event, that idolatry is an old-fashioned sin into which we are never likely to fall. 'Let him who
thinks he stands take heed lest he fall!' We shall do well to
look into our own hearts; the seeds of idolatry are all there.
We should remember the words of Paul: 'Flee from idolatry.'

3. Where is idolatry to be found in the church?

Let me show, in the third place, the forms which idolatry has
assumed, and does assume, in the visible church. Where is it?

I believe there never was a more baseless fabrication than
the theory which obtains favour with many that the promises
of perpetuity and preservation from apostasy belong to the
visible church of Christ [that is, all that is seen among men as
being the church of Christ and called by that name]. It is a
theory supported neither by Scripture nor by facts. The church
against which 'the gates of hell shall never prevail' is not the
visible church, but the whole body of the elect, the company
of true believers out of every nation and people. The greater
part of the visible church has frequently maintained gross heresies. The particular branches of it are never secure against
deadly error, both in matters of faith and practice. A departure
from the faith, a falling away, a leaving of first love in any
branch of the visible church need never surprise a careful reader
of the New Testament.

Idolatry in the church in New Testament times

That idolatry would arise seems to have been expected by the
apostles, even before the canon of the New Testament was

closed. It is remarkable to observe how Paul dwells on this subject in his Epistle to the Corinthians. If any Corinthian who was called a brother was an idolater, the members of the church were 'not even to eat with such a person' (1 Cor. 5:11). 'Do not become idolaters as were some of [our fathers]' (1 Cor. 10:7). He says again, in the text quoted at the head of this chapter, 'My beloved, flee from idolatry' (1 Cor. 10:14). When he writes to the Colossians, he warns them against the 'worship of angels' (Col. 2:18). And John closes his First Epistle with the solemn injunction: 'Little children, keep yourselves from idols' (1 John 5:21). It is impossible not to feel that all these passages imply an expectation that idolatry would arise, and that it would do so soon, among professing Christians.

The famous prophecy in the fourth chapter of the First Epistle to Timothy contains a passage which is even more directly to the point: 'Now the Spirit expressly says that in latter times some will depart from the faith, giving heed to deceiving spirits and doctrines of demons' (1 Tim. 4:1). I will not detain my readers with any lengthy discussion of that remarkable expression, 'doctrines of demons'. It may be sufficient to say that the translators of the Bible are considered for once to have missed the full meaning of the apostle in their rendering of the word translated as 'demons' and that the true meaning of the expression is: 'doctrines about departed spirits'. And according to this view, which, I may as well say, is maintained by those who have the best right to be heard on such a question, the passage becomes a direct prediction of the rise of that most subtle form of idolatry, the worship of dead saints.

The last passage I will call attention to is the conclusion of the ninth chapter of Revelation, where we read, 'The rest of mankind, who were not killed by these plagues, did not repent of the works of their hands, that they should not worship demons' (this is the same word, we should observe, as that in the Epistle to Timothy in the passage just quoted), 'and idols of

gold, silver, brass, stone, and wood, which can neither see nor
hear nor walk' (Rev. 9:20). Now, I am not going to offer any
comment on the chapter in which this verse occurs. I am well
aware that there is a difference of opinion as to the true interpretation of the plagues predicted in it. I only venture to assert
that it is highly probable that these plagues are to fall on the
visible church of Christ, and highly improbable that John was
here prophesying about the heathen who never heard the gospel. And if this is once conceded the fact that idolatry is predicted as *a sin of the visible church* does seem most conclu-
sively and for ever established.

The testimony of history

And now, if we turn from the Bible to facts, what do we see?
I reply unhesitatingly that there is unmistakable proof that
Scripture warnings and predictions were not spoken without
cause, and that idolatry has actually arisen in the visible church
of Christ, and still does exist.

The rise and progress of the evil in former days we shall
find well summed up in the chapter of the Church of England
Book of Homilies on the 'Peril of Idolatry'. (To that chapter I
beg to refer all members of the Anglican Church, reminding
them once for all that, in the judgement of the Thirty-Nine
Articles, the *Book of Homilies* 'contains a godly and wholesome doctrine, and necessary for these times'.)

There we read how, even in *the fourth century*, Jerome
complains that error has 'come in, and passed to the Christians from the Gentiles' over the matter of 'images', and
Eusebius says, 'We see that images of Peter and Paul, and of
our Saviour himself, are made, which I think to have been
derived and kept ... by a heathen custom.'

There too we may also read how Pontius Paulinus, Bishop
of Nola, *in the fifth century,* caused the walls of the temples to

be painted with stories taken out of the Old Testament; that the people, looking at and considering these pictures, might more readily abstain from excess and from riotous behaviour. 'But from learning by painted stories, it came little by little to idolatry.'

There we may also read how Gregory I, Bishop of Rome, at the beginning of *the seventh century*, allowed images to be freely used in churches.

We may read too how Irene, mother of Constantine VI, *in the eighth century,* assembled a council at Nicaea and procured a decree that images should be put up in all the churches of Greece, and that honour and worship should be given to these images.

And there we may read the conclusion with which the chapter winds up its historical summary, stating that clergy and laity alike, educated and uneducated, men, women and children of all ages, of every description and every rank in life throughout the whole of Christendom, have been at once drowned in detestable idolatry, which is of all other vices the most detested by God and the most pernicious to man, and that this had been the case for 800 years or more. This is a mournful account, but it is only too true. There can be little doubt the evil began even before the time mentioned by the writers of the *Book of Homilies*.

No one, I think, need wonder at the rise of idolatry in the early church who considers calmly the excessive reverence which it paid, from the very first, to the outward, visible aspects of religion. I believe that no impartial man can read the language used by nearly all the Fathers about the church, the bishops, the ministry, baptism, the Lord's Supper, the martyrs, the dead saints generally — no man can read it without being struck by the wide difference between their language and the language of Scripture on such subjects. You seem at once to be in a new atmosphere. You feel that you are no longer treading on holy ground. You find that things which in the Bible are evidently of second-rate importance are here made of first-rate importance. You find the things of sense and sight exalted to a position in which Paul, Peter, James and John, speaking by the Holy Spirit, never for a moment placed them. It is not merely the weakness of uninspired writings that you have to complain of; it is something worse; it is a new system.

And what is the explanation of all this? It is, in one word, that you have got into a region where the infection of idolatry has begun to appear. You perceive the first workings of the mystery of lawlessness (2 Thess. 2:7). You detect the first budding of that huge system of idolatry which, as the *Book of Homilies* describes, was afterwards formally acknowledged and ultimately blossomed so profusely in every part of Christendom.

Idolatry in the visible church today

But let us now turn from the past to the present. Let us examine the question which most concerns ourselves. Let us consider in what form idolatry presents itself to us as a sin of the visible church of Christ in our own time. I find no difficulty in answering this question. I feel no hesitation in affirming that idolatry never yet assumed a more glaring form than it does in the Roman Catholic Church in this present day.

And here I come to a subject on which it is hard to speak, because of the times in which we live. But the whole truth ought to be spoken by ministers of Christ, without respect of times and prejudices. And I should not lie down in peace, after writing on idolatry, if I did not declare my solemn conviction that idolatry is one of the crying sins of which the Roman Catholic Church is guilty. I say this in all sadness. I say it, acknowledging fully that we have our faults in the Protestant church and practically, perhaps, in some quarters, a little idolatry. But from formal, recognized, systematic idolatry, I believe we are almost entirely free. While, as for the church of Rome, if there is not in her worship an enormous quantity of systematic, organized idolatry, I frankly confess that I do not know what idolatry is.

In the first place, to my mind, it is idolatry to have images and pictures of saints in churches, and to give them a reverence for which there is no warrant or precedent in Scripture. And if this is the case, I say there is idolatry in the Roman Catholic Church.

Secondly, to my mind, it is idolatry to invoke the Virgin Mary and the saints in glory, and to address them in language never addressed to anyone in Scripture except to the Holy Trinity. And if this is the case, I say there is idolatry in the Roman Catholic Church.

Thirdly, to my mind, it is idolatry to bow down to mere material things and attribute to them a power and sanctity far in excess of that attached to the ark or altar in Old Testament times, and a power and sanctity, too, for which there is not the slightest foundation in the Word of God. And if this is the case, I say, with the holy coat of Trier and the wonderfully multiplied wood of the 'true cross' and a thousand other so-called relics in my mind's eye, that there is idolatry in the Roman Catholic Church.

Fourthly, to my mind, it is idolatry to worship that which man's hands have made — to call it God and adore it when lifted up before our eyes. And if this is so, I say, recalling the notorious doctrine of transubstantiation and the elevation of the host, that there is idolatry in the Roman Catholic Church.

Fifthly, to my mind, it is idolatry to make ordained men mediators between ourselves and God, robbing, as it were,

our Lord Christ of his office, and giving them an honour which
even apostles and angels in Scripture flatly repudiate. And if
this is so, I say, with the honour paid to popes and priests in
view, that there is idolatry in the Roman Catholic Church.

I know very well that language like this jars on the minds of
many. Men love to shut their eyes against evils which it is
disagreeable to have to acknowledge. They will not see things
which involve unpleasant consequences. That the Roman
Catholic Church is in error, they will acknowledge. That she is
idolatrous, they will deny.

They tell us that the reverence which the church of Rome
gives to saints and images does not amount to idolatry. They
inform us that there are distinctions between the worship of
'latria' and 'dulia',[2] between a mediation of redemption and a
mediation of intercession, which clear her of the charge. My
answer is that the Bible knows nothing of such distinctions
and that, in the actual practice of the great majority of Roman
Catholics, they have no existence at all.

They tell us that it is a mistake to suppose that Roman
Catholics really worship the images and pictures before which
they perform acts of adoration, that they only use them as
helps to devotion, and in reality look far beyond them. My
answer is that many a pagan could say just as much for his
idolatry, that it is well-known that, in former days, they did
say so and that in the Indian sub-continent many idol-worshippers do say so at the present day. But the apology does
not help. The terms of the second commandment are too stringent. It prohibits bowing down, as well as worshipping. And
the very anxiety which the Roman Catholic Church has often
displayed to exclude that second commandment from her

2. 'Latria' and 'dulia' are two Greek words, both meaning 'worship' or 'service', but the former is a much stronger word than the latter. The Roman Catholic
admits that the worship of 'latria' may not be given to saints, but maintains that
'dulia' may be given.

catechisms is of itself a great fact which speaks volumes to a candid observer.

They tell us that we have no evidence for the assertions we make on this subject, that we found our charges on the abuses which prevail among the ignorant members of the Roman communion and that it is absurd to say that a church containing so many wise and learned men is guilty of idolatry. My answer is that the devotional books in common use among Roman Catholics supply us with unmistakable evidence. Let anyone examine that well-known book, *The Garden of the Soul,* if he doubts my assertion, and read the language addressed there to the Virgin Mary. Let him remember that this language is addressed to a woman who, though highly favoured, and the mother of our Lord, was yet one of our fellow-sinners — to a woman, who actually confesses her need of a Saviour for herself. She says, 'My spirit has rejoiced in God my Saviour' (Luke 1:47). Let him examine this language in the light of the New Testament, and then let him tell us fairly, whether the charge of idolatry is not correctly made.

But I answer, beside this, that we want no better evidence than that which is supplied in the city of Rome itself. What do men and women do before the very eyes of the pope and with his approval? What is the religion that prevails around St Peter's and under the walls of the Vatican? What is Roman Catholicism at Rome, unfettered, unshackled and free to develop itself fully and completely? Let a man honestly answer these questions, and I ask no more. Let him read such a book as Seymour's *Pilgrimage to Rome* or Alford's *Letters*, and ask any visitor to Rome if the picture is too highly coloured. Let him do this, I say, and I believe he cannot avoid the conclusion that Roman Catholicism when fully developed is a gigantic system of worship of churches, worship of the sacrament, worship of Mary, worship of saints, worship of images, worship of relics and worship of priests — that it is, in one word, a huge, organized system of idolatry.

I know how painful these things sound to many ears. To me it is no pleasure to dwell on the shortcomings of any who profess to be, and call themselves, Christians. I can truly say that I have said what I have said with pain and sorrow.

I draw a wide distinction between the accredited dogmas of the Roman Catholic Church and the private opinions of many of her members. I believe and hope that many a Roman Catholic is in heart inconsistent with his profession and is better than the church to which he belongs. I cannot forget the Jansenists and others who sought to reform the church from within. I believe that many a poor Italian is worshipping with an idolatrous worship simply because he knows no better. He has no Bible to instruct him. He has no faithful minister to teach him. He has the fear of the priest before his eyes, if he dares to think for himself. He has no money to enable him to get away from the bondage he lives under, even if he feels a desire to do so. I remember all this, and I say that the Italian eminently deserves our sympathy and compassion. But all this must not prevent my saying that the Roman Catholic Church is an idolatrous church.

I should not be faithful if I said less. The church of which I am a minister has spoken out most strongly on the subject. The chapter in the *Book of Homilies* on the 'Peril of Idolatry' quoted earlier and the solemn protest at the end of the Prayer Book communion service which denounces the adoration of the bread and wine used in the sacrament as 'idolatry to be abhorred of all faithful Christians', are plain evidence that I have said no more than the mind of my own church. And in a day like this, when some are disposed to leave the church to join the Roman Catholic Church and many are shutting their eyes to her real character, and wanting us to be reunited to her — in a day like this, my own conscience would rebuke me if I did not warn men plainly that the church of Rome is an idolatrous church, and that if they will join her they are 'joining themselves to idols'.

But I will not dwell any longer on this part of my subject. The main point I wish to impress on men's minds is this — that idolatry has decidedly manifested itself in the visible church of Christ, and nowhere so decidedly as in the Roman Catholic Church.

4. What will put an end to idolatry in the visible church?

And now let me show, in the last place, the ultimate abolition of all idolatry. What will put an end to it? I consider that the soul of any man who does not long for the time when idolatry shall be no more must be in an unhealthy state. That heart can hardly be right with God which can think of the millions who are sunk in the worship of false gods, or who honour the false prophet Mohammed, or who daily offer up prayers to the Virgin Mary, and which does not cry, 'O my God, what will put an end to these things? How long, O Lord, how long?'

Here, as in other subjects, the sure word of prophecy comes in to our aid. The end of all idolatry will come one day. Its doom is fixed. Its overthrow is certain. Whether in pagan temples, or in so-called Christian churches, idolatry will be destroyed at the Second Coming of our Lord Jesus Christ.

Then the prophecy of Isaiah will be fulfilled: 'The idols he shall utterly abolish' (Isa. 2:18). Then the words of Micah will be fulfilled: 'Your carved images I will also cut off, and your sacred pillars from your midst; you shall no more worship the work of your hands' (Micah 5:13). The prophecy of Zephaniah will be fulfilled: 'The Lord will be awesome to them, for he will reduce to nothing all the gods of the earth; people shall worship him, each one from his place, indeed all the shores of the nations' (Zeph. 2:11). The prophecy of Zechariah will be fulfilled: ' "It shall be in that day," says the Lord of hosts, "that I will cut off the names of the idols from the land, and they shall no longer be remembered" ' (Zech. 13:2).

In a word, what is described in the 97th Psalm will then be accomplished in full:

The LORD reigns;
Let the earth rejoice;
Let the multitude of isles be glad!
Clouds and darkness surround him;
Righteousness and justice are the foundation of his throne.
A fire goes before him,
And burns up his enemies round about.
His lightnings light the world;
The earth sees and trembles.
The mountains melt like wax at the presence of the LORD,
At the presence of the Lord of the whole earth.
The heavens declare his righteousness,
And all the peoples see his glory.
Let all be put to shame who serve carved images,
Who boast of idols.
Worship him, all you gods

(Ps. 97:1-7).

The Second Coming of our Lord Jesus Christ is the blessed hope which should always comfort the children of God in the present age. It is the pole-star by which we must navigate. It is the one point on which all our expectations should be concentrated. 'For yet a little while, and he who is coming will come and will not tarry' (Heb. 10:37). Our David will no longer live in the Cave of Adullam, followed by a despised few and rejected by the many. He will take to himself his great power and reign, and cause every knee to bow before him.

Till then *our redemption is not perfectly enjoyed*. As Paul tells the Ephesians, 'You were sealed for the day of redemption' (Eph. 4:30). Till then *our salvation is not completed*. As Peter says, we 'are kept by the power of God through faith for salvation ready to be revealed in the last time' (1 Peter 1:5). Till then *our knowledge is still defective.* As Paul tells the Corinthians, 'Now we see in a mirror, dimly, but then face to face. Now I know in part, but then I shall know just as I also am known' (1 Cor. 13:12). In short, our best things are yet to come.

But in the day of our Lord's return every desire will receive its fulfilment. We shall no longer be pressed down and worn out with the sense of constant failure, feebleness and disappointment. In his presence we shall find there is a fulness of joy, if we found it nowhere else; and when we wake up in his likeness we shall be satisfied, if we never were before (Ps. 16:11; 17:15).

There are many evils now in the visible church, over which we can only sigh and cry, like the faithful in Ezekiel's day (Ezek. 9:4). We cannot remove them. The wheat and the weeds will grow together until the harvest. But a day is coming when the Lord Jesus will once more purify his temple and cast out everything that defiles. He will do that work of which the actions of Hezekiah and Josiah long ago were a faint type. He will cast out the images and purge out idolatry in every shape.

Who is there now that longs for the conversion of the unbelieving world? You will not see it in its fulness until the Lord's appearing. Then, and not till then, will that text be fulfilled which has so often been wrongly applied:

In that day a man will cast away his idols of silver
And his idols of gold,
Which they made, each for himself to worship,
To the moles and the bats

(Isa. 2:20).

Who is there now that longs for the redemption of Israel? You will never see it in its perfection till the Redeemer comes to Zion. Idolatry in the professing church of Christ has been one of the mightiest stumbling blocks in the Jew's way. When it begins to fall, the veil over the heart of Israel will begin to be taken away (Ps. 102:16).

Who is there now that longs for the fall of Antichrist and the purification of the Roman Catholic Church? I believe that will never be until the winding up of this age. That vast system of idolatry may be consumed and laid waste by the Spirit of the Lord's mouth, but it will never be destroyed except by the brightness of his coming (2 Thess. 2:8).

Who is there now that longs for a perfect church — a church in which there will not be the slightest taint of idolatry? You must wait for the Lord's return. Then, and not till then, shall we see a perfect church — a church having neither spot nor wrinkle, nor any such thing (Eph. 5:27) — a church of which all the members will be truly born again and every one a child of God.

If these things are so, men need not wonder that we urge on them the study of prophecy and that we charge them above all to grasp firmly the glorious doctrine of Christ's second appearing and kingdom. This is the 'light that shines in a dark place' which we shall 'do well to heed'. Let others indulge their fancy if they will with the vision of an imaginary 'church of the future'. Let the people of this world dream of some man who will come, who is to understand everything and set everything right. They are only sowing to themselves bitter disappointment. They will awake to find their visions without foundation and empty as a dream. It is to such as these that the prophet's words may well be applied:

Look, all you who kindle a fire,
Who encircle yourselves with sparks:
Walk in the light of your fire and in the sparks you have
    kindled —

This you shall have from my hand:
You shall lie down in torment

(Isa. 50:11).

But let your eyes look onward to the day of Christ's second advent. That is the only day when every abuse shall be rectified and every corruption and source of sorrow completely purged away. Waiting for that day, let us each work on and serve our generation — not idle, as if nothing could be done to check evil, but not disheartened because we do not yet see all things put under our Lord. After all, the night is almost over and the day is at hand. Let us wait, I say, on the Lord.

If these things are so, men need not wonder that we warn them to beware of all leanings towards the Roman Catholic Church. Surely, when the mind of God about idolatry is so plainly revealed to us in his Word, it seems the height of infatuation in anyone to join a church so steeped in idolatries as the church of Rome. To enter into communion with her, when God is saying, 'Come out of her, my people, lest you share in her sins, and lest you receive of her plagues' (Rev. 18:4), to seek her when the Lord is warning us to leave her, to become her subjects when the Lord's voice is crying, 'Escape for your life! Flee from the wrath to come!' — all this is mental blindness indeed, a blindness like that of the one who, though forewarned, embarks in a sinking ship — a blindness which would be almost incredible, if our own eyes did not see examples of it continually.

We must all be on our guard. We must take nothing for granted. We must not hastily suppose that we are too wise to be ensnared and say like Hazael, 'But what is your servant — a dog, that he should do this gross thing?' (2 Kings 8:13). Those who preach must cry aloud and spare not, and allow no false tenderness to make them hold their peace about the heresies of the day. Those who hear must have their waist girded with truth (Eph. 6:14), and their minds stored with clear prophetical views of the end to which all idol-worshippers must come. Let us all try to realize that the final days of the world are close at hand, and that the time is hurrying on when all idolatry shall be abolished. Is this a time for a man to draw nearer to Rome? Is it not rather a time to draw further back and stand clear, so that we are not involved in her downfall? Is this a time to plead extenuating circumstances for, and gloss over, Rome's numerous corruptions, and refuse to see the reality of her sins? Surely we ought rather to be doubly jealous in guarding against everything in religion that tends towards Romanism, doubly careful that we are not guilty of conniving at any treason against our Lord Christ and doubly ready to protest against unscriptural worship of every description. Once more, then, I say, let us remember that the destruction of all idolatry is certain and, remembering that, beware of the church of Rome.

The subject I now touch upon is of deep and pressing importance, and demands the serious attention of all members of Protestant churches. It is vain to deny that a large party of both clergymen and lay people in the present day are moving heaven and earth to reunite the Church of England with the idolatrous Roman Catholic Church. The existence of such a movement as this will not surprise anyone who has carefully watched the history of the Church of England over the years. The tendency of the Oxford Movement[3] and of ritualism has been steadily towards Rome. Hundreds of men and women have fairly and honestly left the ranks of the Anglican Church

---

3. The Oxford Movement was a movement in the mid-nineteenth century, led by a group of men based at Oxford, which aimed at restoring traditional Roman Catholic teaching in the Church of England and formed the basis for the development of Anglo-Catholicism.

and openly become Roman Catholics. But many hundreds more have stayed behind, and are still nominal Anglicans. The pompous ceremonial, verging on that of Roman Catholicism, which has been introduced into many churches, has prepared men's minds for changes. An extravagantly theatrical and idolatrous mode of celebrating the Lord's Supper has paved the way for transubstantiation. A regular process of removing the distinctive marks of Protestantism has been long and successfully at work. The poor old Church of England stands on a downward slope. Her very existence, as a Protestant church, is in peril.

I hold, for one, that this movement towards Rome ought to be steadily and firmly resisted. Notwithstanding the rank, the learning and the devotedness of some of its advocates, I regard it as a soul-ruining and unscriptural movement that is likely to cause serious harm. To say that reunion with Rome would be an insult to our martyred Reformers is a very light thing; it is far more than this: it would be a sin and an offence against God! Rather than be reunited with the idolatrous church of Rome, I would willingly see my own beloved church perish and go to pieces. Rather than become Roman Catholic once more, she had better die!

Unity in the abstract is no doubt an excellent thing, but unity without truth is useless. Peace and uniformity are beautiful and valuable, but peace without the gospel — peace based on a common recognition of each other's ministry and not on a common faith — is a worthless peace, not deserving of the name. When Rome has repealed the decrees of the Council of Trent and her additions to the Creed, when Rome has recanted her false and unscriptural doctrines, when Rome has formally renounced the worship of images, the worship of Mary and transubstantiation — then, and not till then, it will be time to talk of reunion with her. Till then there is a gulf between us which cannot be honestly bridged. Till then I call on all loyal members of the church to resist to the death this idea of reunion with Rome. Till then let our watchwords be: 'No peace with Rome! No communion with idolaters!' Bishop Jewell well says, in his *Apology*, 'We do not decline concord and peace with men; but we will not continue in a state of war with God that we might have peace with men! If the pope does indeed desire we should be reconciled to him, he ought first to reconcile himself to God.' This witness is true! It would have been a good thing for the Church of England if all her bishops had been like Jewell!

I write these things with sorrow. But the circumstances of the times make it absolutely necessary to speak out. To whatever quarter of the horizon I turn, I see grave reason for alarm. For the true church of Christ I have no fears at all. But for the established Church of England and for all the Protestant churches of Great Britain, I have very grave fears indeed. The tide of events seems running strongly against Protestantism and in favour of Rome. It looks as if God had a controversy with us, as a nation, and was about to punish us for our sins.

I am no prophet. I do not know where we are drifting. But at the rate we are going, I think it quite possible that in a few years the Church of England may be reunited to the Roman Catholic Church. A Roman Catholic may once more sit on the throne and Protestantism may be formally repudiated. A Roman Catholic archbishop may once more preside in Lambeth Palace.[4] Mass may once more be said at Westminster Abbey and St Paul's. And one result will be that all Bible-reading Christians must either leave the Church of England, or else sanction idol-worship and become idolaters! May God grant we may never come to this state of things! But at the rate we are going, it seems to me quite possible.

---

4. The official residence of the Archbishop of Canterbury.

Words of advice to the reader

And now it only remains for me to conclude what I have been
saying by mentioning some safeguards for the souls of all who
read this book. We live in a time when Roman Catholicism is
walking amongst us with renewed strength and loudly boast-
ing that she will soon win back the ground that she has lost.
False doctrines of every kind are continually set before us in
the most subtle and beguiling forms. It cannot be thought
inappropriate if I offer some practical safeguards against idolatry. What it is, where it comes from, where it is, what will
bring it to an end — all this we have seen. Let me point out
how we may be safe from it, and I will say no more.

1. A thorough knowledge of the Word of God

Let us arm ourselves, then, for one thing, with a thorough
knowledge of the Word of God. Let us read our Bibles more
diligently than ever, and become familiar with every part of
them. Let the Word dwell in us richly. Let us beware of anything which would make us give less time, and less heart, to
the perusal of its sacred pages. The Bible is the sword of the
Spirit; let it never be laid aside. The Bible is the true lantern
for a dark and cloudy time; let us beware of travelling without
its light. I strongly suspect that if we only knew the secret
history of the numerous secessions from the Anglican Church
to that of Rome, which we deplore — I strongly suspect that
in almost every case one of the most important steps in the
downward road would be found to have been a neglected Bible
— more attention to outward forms of worship, sacraments,
daily services, the early church, and so on, and diminished
attention to the written Word of God. The Bible is the King's
highway. If we once leave that for any alternative route,

however beautiful and old and frequented it may seem, we must never be surprised if we end up worshipping images and relics and going regularly to confession.

2. A godly jealousy for the gospel

Let us arm ourselves, in the second place, with a godly jealousy to see that no part of the gospel, however small, is lost. Let us beware of sanctioning the slightest attempt to keep back even the smallest detail of it, or to throw any part of it into the shade by exalting subordinate matters in religion. When Peter withdrew himself from eating with the Gentiles, it seemed only a little thing, yet Paul tells the Galatians, 'I withstood him to his face, because he was to be blamed' (Gal. 2:11). Let us count nothing little that concerns our souls. Let us be very particular whom we hear, where we go and what we do, in all the matters of our own particular worship, and let us not worry about people calling us hard to please or over-scrupulous. We live in days when great principles are involved in little acts, and things in religion which in an earlier age were matters of indifference are now by circumstances rendered no longer matters of indifference. Let us beware of tampering with anything which tends towards Roman Catholicism. It is foolishness to play with fire. I believe that many of those who turned away from the faith and left the church began with thinking there could be no great harm in attaching *a little* more importance to certain outward things than they once did. But once launched on the downward course, they went on from one thing to another. They provoked God, and he left them to themselves! They were given over to strong delusion, and allowed to believe a lie (2 Thess. 2:11). They tempted the devil, and he came to them! They started with trifles, as many foolishly call them. They have ended with downright idolatry.

3. Clear, sound views of Christ and his work

Let us arm ourselves, last of all, with clear, sound views of our
Lord Jesus Christ, and of the salvation that is in him.

He is 'the image of the invisible God', 'the express image
of his person' and the true preservative against all idolatry,
when truly known. Let us build ourselves deep down on the
strong foundation of his finished work upon the cross. Let us
settle it firmly in our minds that Christ Jesus has done everything necessary in order to present us without spot before the
throne of God, and that simple, childlike faith on our part is
the only thing required to give us an entire interest in the work
of Christ. Let us not doubt that, having this faith, we are completely justified in the sight of God; that we shall never be
more justified than we are now, if we live to the age of
Methuselah and do the works of the apostle Paul; and that we
can add nothing to that complete justification by any acts,
deeds, words, performances, fasting, prayers, giving to those
in need, attendance on ordinances, or anything else of our own.

Above all, let us keep up continual communion with the
person of the Lord Jesus! Let us abide in him daily, feed on
him daily, look to him daily, lean on him daily, live upon him
daily, draw from his fulness daily. Let us realize this, and the
idea of other mediators, other comforters, other intercessors,
will seem utterly absurd. 'What need is there?' we shall reply.
'I have Christ, and in him I have all. What have I to do with
idols? I have Jesus in my heart, Jesus in the Bible and Jesus in
heaven, and I want nothing more!'

Once let the Lord Christ have his rightful place in our hearts,
and all other things in our religion will soon fall into their right
places — church, ministers, sacraments, ordinances — all will
go down and take the second place.

Unless Christ sits as Priest and King upon the throne of our
hearts, that little kingdom within us will be in perpetual

confusion. But only let him be 'all in all' there, and all will be well. Before him every idol, every Dagon, shall fall down (see 1 Sam. 5:1-5). Christ rightly known, Christ truly believed and Christ heartily loved is the true preservative against ritualism, Romanism and every form of idolatry.